English Reading for Academic Purposes

A Course Book for Graduate Students
of Humanities and Social Sciences

研究生学术英语阅读

人文类

总主编 陈新仁 黄 燕
主 编 朱 适 韩戈玲
副主编 于 江
编 者 朱 适 韩戈玲
　　　　于 江 曾 姝
　　　　张豪若

清华大学出版社
北京

内 容 简 介

《研究生学术英语阅读：人文类》是"研究生学术英语实用教程"系列教材之一。本教材面向研究生阅读学术英语文献的现实需求，细致呈现学术英语体裁，尤其是人文社科类学术论文的结构特征和语言特点，旨在培养研究生的学术英语文本阅读技能和反思能力。与同类教材相比，本教材更具系统性和操作性，支持研究型学习，可以满足研究生和高年级本科生快速、有效提升学术阅读能力的需求。

本教材另配有练习的答案详解，读者可登录 ftp: ftp.tup.tsinghua.edu.cn/ 下载使用。

版权所有，侵权必究。举报：010-62782989，beiqinquan@tup.tsinghua.edu.cn。

图书在版编目（CIP）数据

研究生学术英语阅读：人文类 / 陈新仁，黄燕总主编；朱适，韩戈玲主编. —北京：清华大学出版社，2022.6
ISBN 978-7-302-60918-6

Ⅰ. ①研… Ⅱ. ①陈… ②黄… ③朱… ④韩… Ⅲ. ①英语—阅读教学—研究生—教材 Ⅳ. ① H319.4

中国版本图书馆 CIP 数据核字（2022）第 088662 号

责任编辑：方燕贝　刘　艳
封面设计：李尘工作室
责任校对：王凤芝
责任印制：曹婉颖

出版发行：清华大学出版社
网　　址：http://www.tup.com.cn, http://www.wqbook.com
地　　址：北京清华大学学研大厦 A 座　　邮　编：100084
社 总 机：010-83470000　　邮　购：010-62786544
投稿与读者服务：010-62776969, c-service@tup.tsinghua.edu.cn
质量反馈：010-62772015, zhiliang@tup.tsinghua.edu.cn

印 装 者：大厂回族自治县彩虹印刷有限公司
经　　销：全国新华书店
开　　本：185mm×260mm　　印　张：10.75　　字　数：210 千字
版　　次：2022 年 8 月第 1 版　　印　次：2022 年 8 月第 1 次印刷
定　　价：59.00 元

产品编号：095240-01

总　序

研究生教育肩负着国家高层次人才培养和创新创造的重要使命，是国家发展、社会进步的重要基石。研究生英语课程对于持续提高研究生的人文素养和专业能力，培养学生的家国情怀和创新精神，引导学生坚定文化自信、学术自信，成为有理想、有国际学术视野的高层次、创新性人才，从而更好地服务于国家的发展战略，都具有不可替代的重要作用。

为贯彻落实教育部印发的《高等学校课程思政建设指导纲要》，彰显立德树人根本宗旨，培养研究生的学术英语能力和跨文化交流能力，深入推进新时代研究生培养国际化，我们秉持以学生学习为中心的教育学理念，结合我国研究生英语学习实际需求和教学现状，策划编写了本套"研究生学术英语实用教程"系列教材，由《研究生学术英语阅读：理工类》《研究生学术英语阅读：人文类》《研究生学术英语写作：理工类》《研究生学术英语写作：人文类》《研究生学术英语视听说》共五册教材构成。

本套教材的编写原则与思路如下：

一、以立德树人为总目标，秉承以学生发展为中心、以学生学习为中心的理念，两个中心相辅相成，互为支撑。以学生发展为中心体现在将思政教育有机融入教材设计中，内容选择与问题设计体现中国学术贡献、学术诚信、文化自信、科学素养等思政元素。以学生学习为中心体现在内容设计围绕真实的学术活动展开，满足学生用英语进行专业学习、开展国际学术交流的现实需要。

二、着眼于跨文化学术交际，体现国际化人才培养的定位。本套教材将学术交流置于跨文化语境之中，注重培养学生的国际视野和跨文化学术交际意识，提升跨文化沟通中所需的学术交流能力和思辨能力。一方面，各分册的选材都能兼顾中外学者、中英文学术语篇，提供比较分析的机会。另一方面，各分册所选语料都蕴含具体的学术体裁知识，为学生习得跨文化学术交流所需的各种学术英语知识提供必要的支持。

三、本着"在用中学"的编写理念，着力于学生多元能力培养。新时代深化研究生培养改革，必须着力增强研究生实践能力、创新能力等多元能力的培养。本套教材强调能力培养至上而非知识传授至上。各分册采用"以项目为导向"的学术英语教学方法，注重实际学术活动的参与和体验，以输入驱动输出，将听、说、读、写、译五项语言技能有机融合，强调综合语言应用能力、合作学习、自主学习能力的培养，激励学生通过讨论及修改反例等练习形式提升批判性思辨能力。

四、体现学术共性与学科差异。基于大类学科（如理工类、人文类）的特点，设计各分册，每个分册选材真实地道，来源多样，内涵丰富。同一单元涵盖多门学科，体现大学科特色，以支撑高校主流学科国际化人才的培养。

五、体现信息技术支撑。为实现教材编写目标，培养学生的自主学习能力，本套教材在各分册中都设计了让学生利用互联网自主查找文献或相关资源的教学活动。另外，全套教材采用线上与线下相结合的方式提供课堂教学资源和拓展学习资源。

本着上述编写原则和思路，"研究生学术英语实用教程"系列教材形成以下鲜明特色：

- **育人性**。各分册每个单元都有课程思政的元素，全套教材强调学术诚信和科学素养，力求将育人寓于学术英语知识传授和多元能力培养之中。

- **实用性**。全套教材所选语料来源于真实学术活动，内容设计贴近学生实际阅读、写作、听说需求，为其英语学习提供全面、切实、有效的指导。

- **针对性**。全套教材面向国内非英语专业研究生，在整个编写过程中，以学生为中心，关注他们的实际需求，聚焦他们在学习过程中的重难点，力求合理把握教学内容的难度，为学生提供丰富的、可学可用的语料。

- **可操作性**。全套教材练习形式多样，采用结对练习、小组讨论等形式凸显互动性和合作性，强调获得感。各分册均由八个单元构成，可满足 16 个标准课堂学时的教学需要，服务课堂操作。

作为体现学术共性与学科差异的学术英语系列教材，本套教材可以满足不同院校、不同学科研究生英语教学的需要。我们诚挚欢迎广大英语教师和各位学生在使用本套教材的过程中，能以各种方式提供反馈意见和建议，以便我们不断完善，打造一套启智润心、增知强能的系列精品教材！

陈新仁、黄燕
2022 年 4 月

前　言

《研究生学术英语阅读：人文类》是"研究生学术英语实用教程"系列教材之一。在具体呈现整套教材立德树人的编写理念、思路与特色的基础上，本教材旨在满足我国人文社科研究生进行学术阅读的现实需要。为此，本教材聚焦于学术英语阅读，旨在通过各类体裁的学术英语文本阅读训练，着力提升研究生获得学术英语知识与掌握学术英语相关技能的能力，并在此基础上增强其学术英语的写作、交谈、讨论等能力。

本册特色

本教材充分展现学术英语体裁尤其是人文社科类学术论文的结构特征，详细介绍此类学术体裁文本的语言特点，旨在培养和训练人文社科类研究生通用学术英语阅读和撰写学术英语文本的能力，以期提高其学术表达的规范性，强化学术素养和学术意识，从而为学术研究打好语言基础。作为研究生的学术英语阅读教材，本教材具有独特的整体性、系统性和创新性，适合研究生以及高年级本科生进行较为系统的学术阅读技能的学习。

教材构成

本教材以学科为基础，节选近期发表的、影响力较大的学科期刊论文，共设八个单元，涉及会议征文及手册、论文标题及摘要、论文前言、文献综述、理论呈现及分析、论文结论、审稿人意见及主编决定等内容。每个单元的主体内容由五个板块构成：第一板块为 Part I Introducing the Unit，重点介绍本单元的学习内容和学术能力培养目标；第二板块为 Part II Reading for Expressions，列举介绍学术论文中常用的学术表达与重点短语；第三板块为 Part III Reading for Ideas，设置的思考问题有助于学生熟悉单元话题和背景知识，从而培养其学术文本分析能力和思辨能力；第四板块为 Part IV Reading for Speaking，要求学生在阅读完学术论文后，通过理性思考来讨论与学术论文结构有关的问题，培养其学术英语口语表达能力；第五板块为 Part V Reading for Writing，培养学生恰当使用学术语言撰写学术英语论文的能力。之后还设有 Exercises 和 Project 两个板块，前者主要帮助学生积累并掌握常用的学术短语，巩固对学术论文结构的理解，培养和提高学生判断信息、分析信息和综述信息的能力；后者则重点培养学生利用所学的阅读技能解决实际问题的能力。

教学建议

每个单元的七个板块组成一个有机的整体。Part I 和 Part II 为课前阅读内容，要求学生课前完成，教师可以在课堂上进行检查；Part III、Part IV 和 Part V 为课堂操练内容，教师可以采用各种互动形式，让学生进行全面、有效的练习，并在课堂上及时给予学生反馈；Exercises 板块为课后练习，主要由学生课后独立完成，教师负责及时答疑；Project 板块供学生进行课外的团队学习和项目练习，并在完成后在下一次课上与全班分享。建议每四个课时教授一个单元，教师也可以根据具体情况灵活进行课堂安排。

编写分工

本教材由朱适、韩戈玲担任主编，于江担任副主编，曾姝、张豪若参与编写。各单元的分工情况如下：韩戈玲负责第一单元；于江负责第二、第三单元；朱适负责第四单元；张豪若负责第五、第六单元；曾姝负责第七、第八单元。陈新仁教授和黄燕教授作为总主编，负责审阅、修改和润色文稿。

由于编者水平有限，书中难免存在疏漏和错误之处，敬请广大同仁和英语学习者不吝批评指正。

编者
2022 年 5 月

Contents

Unit 1 **Calls for Papers and Conference Programs** ········1

Unit 2 **Titles and Abstracts** ················29

Unit 3 **Introductions** ··················49

Unit 4 **Literature Reviews** ···············67

Unit 5 **Theoretical Descriptions** ············83

Unit 6 **Theoretical Analyses** ··············99

Unit 7 **Conclusions** ···················117

Unit 8 **Reviewers' Comments and Editors' Decisions** ·······135

References ·······················161

Unit 1

Calls for Papers and Conference Programs

Part I
Introducing the Unit

In this unit, we will learn how to read calls for papers and conference programs, a necessary step for a researcher to attend an academic conference to present his or her research findings or to publish a paper in an academic journal or an edited volume. A call for papers informs the prospective participants of specific information about the academic conference, including the title, date, place, organizer(s) or host(s), sponsor(s), themes, and major topics of the conference. It also provides detailed information about the requirements for the preparation of abstracts and full papers, the deadline of abstract or full paper submission, activity arrangements, chairs and members of the program committee, plenary speakers, the date(s) of conference notice, contact channels, and so on. Sometimes there may be a second call for papers and/or the final call for papers followed. Also, a call for papers can be initiated by the editorial board to address a designated topic for a special issue of a journal or an edited book. In addition, a conference program provides guidance for the participants with a timetable of activities. It usually lists specific information items at great length, including the agenda, venue, and time schedule of various sessions, logistics, and other facilities, so that the participants will be able to attend the conference with convenience.

In the following parts, we will read some samples of calls for papers and conference programs, illustrate their objectives and requirements, and discuss different formats of designing calls for papers and conference programs.

After finishing this unit, you are expected to achieve the following learning objectives:

- to comprehend the essential information in calls for papers and conference programs;
- to use signal phrases and typical templates in writing different calls for papers and conference programs;
- to be familiar with the procedures of abstract or full paper submission to academic conferences;
- to respond to conference invitations and register for academic conferences;
- to deal with a call for papers for a special issue of a journal or an edited book.

Unit 1 Calls for Papers and Conference Programs

Part II
Reading for Expressions

Study the bold-faced expressions that are often used in calls for papers and conference programs.

A. Issuing a Call for Papers

- We would like to **invite you to submit to** FinSIM-3, the 3rd shared task on Learning Semantic Similarities for the Financial Domain.
- We **invite submissions to** the 2021 International Conference on Learning Representations, and **welcome paper submissions** from all areas of machine learning and deep learning.
- The Council for European Studies at Columbia University **invites proposal submissions** for the 28th International Conference of Europeanists **on the theme of** "The Environment of Democracy".
- We sincerely **invite you to take part in** the 2021 11th International Conference on Languages, Literature and Linguistics in Tsuru University, Japan during November 5–7, 2021.
- We **invite** papers on **original, unpublished work** in the topic areas of the workshop. In addition to long papers, we will **consider** short papers and system descriptions (demos). We also **welcome** position papers.
- We **are especially interested in** papers/panels that address one or more aspects of the conference theme, both broadly and specifically.

B. Introducing the Academic Conference or Journal

- We **are pleased to announce** the call for papers for the 5th International Conference of the American Pragmatics Association, held on October 16–18, 2020 at the University of British Columbia in Vancouver, Canada.
- The symposium on "The Disability Gaze: Material and Visual Approaches" will **take place** on April 29–30, 2022, **virtually and in-person** at the University of Delaware.
- Depling is a bi-annual conference **dedicated to** dependency-based approaches in linguistics and natural language processing. Papers should describe original work **related to** dependency-based linguistics. The conference **seeks**, through an interdisciplinary and material culture

approach, **to** reclaim the disability gaze as it extends into lived experience.

- *Glocalism*, a **peer-reviewed, open-access and cross-disciplinary** journal, is currently **accepting manuscripts for publication**.

C. Stating the Submission Policy

- Submissions will **be judged on** correctness, originality, technical strength, significance and relevance to the conference, and interest to the attendees.
- Submissions **are limited to** one individual and one joint abstract per author, or two joint abstracts per author, and papers **must be** in English.
- Submitted papers should be **at most** 12 pages long, with one additional page for references, in PDF format **following the Springer LNCS (Lecture Notes in Computer Science) style**.
- Inquiries concerning the submission of papers should **be addressed to** Dr. Meyer.
- Authors have the right to **withdraw papers** from consideration at any time until paper notification.
- Submitted papers that do not **conform to** these policies will **be rejected** without review.
- **It is not appropriate to** submit papers that are **identical** (or substantially similar) **to** versions that have been previously published, accepted for publication, or submitted **in parallel** to other conferences or journals.
- Submissions **violate our dual submission policy**, and the organizers **have the right to** reject such submissions, or to **remove them from** the proceedings.
- International Conference on Machine Learning strongly discourages **advertising the preprint** on social media or in the press while under submission to ICML.
- All submissions **must be anonymized** and **may not contain** any information with the intention or consequence of violating the double-blind reviewing policy.
- Authors should **include a full title** for their paper, as well as a complete abstract by the abstract submission deadline.
- All papers will **be reviewed in a double-blind process** and accepted papers will **be presented** at the conference.
- Please note that **priority will be given to** full panel submissions.

Unit 1 Calls for Papers and Conference Programs

- To **submit** an abstract for the conference, please **go to the following link**.
- The **early submission deadline** has been **extended to** March 5, 2020.

D. Notifying the Conference Program

- The main session of 49th Linguistic Symposium on Romance Languages will **consist of** oral presentations and two poster sessions.
- Programming will include paper presentations, panels, **round table discussions**, and expert keynote speakers from Israel and abroad.
- In-person conference participants can **join the virtual conference** as "observers" **free of charge**.
- In addition, **registered in-person participants** may **act as** chair, moderator, or discussant for one additional virtual session.
- The Program Committee **has final authority over** which papers will be included in each panel.
- Panel sessions will **be scheduled for** no more than two time-slots (2 × 90).

E. Providing Information for Registration, Accommodation, and Sponsorship

- Interested parties are kindly requested to **register in advance**.
- Acceptance of abstract **is based on** payment of conference registration fee.
- When you **are notified of** your proposal acceptance via e-mail, the conference organizers will **provide you with** information about registration payment, hotel, transportation, and other related information.
- Participants **are responsible for** paying the conference **non-refundable early bird registration fee** of $125.00(per person), payable upon the acceptance of their proposal and as a condition of the inclusion in the conference preliminary program in February 2022.
- The conference organizer will **provide accommodation for** all selected participants. If necessary, **travel expenses** may also be covered up to $1,000.
- The symposium **is sponsored by** the Foundazione Gravissimum Educationis, Rome.

Part III
Reading for Ideas

The following two passages are related to how to write a call for papers and how it presents information. Read the passages and answer the questions to understand the main ideas of each passage.

Passage A

A call for papers (CFP) is the document sent out to seek academic papers for a conference, a special issue of a journal, or an edited volume. Here, we share five tips on how to write a call for papers.

First, start with information about the academic event or publication.

Describe what the conference or publication will be about, including some key information:

- the title, date, and location of a conference;
- name of the journal, members of the editors, and the title of a special issue of the journal;
- title and editors of an edited volume.

This information will give readers an immediate sense of whether the CFP is appropriate for them.

Next, describe what are requested.

Make clear what kinds of papers are requested. You need to describe the overall themes of the conference or publication and list the topics the editors or organizers are most interested in.

And then, explain the submission process.

Usually, a call for papers will ask researchers to submit a writing proposal along with a CV or a short biography. You should specify how long the proposal should be and what form it should take. For example, some CFPs ask for an abstract of around 250 words. It's also a good idea to ask for CVs to be no more than one or two pages

Unit 1 Calls for Papers and Conference Programs

long, especially if you are expecting many submissions.

In addition, you need to explain how scholars should submit their proposals—should they e-mail them? Or is there an online form they should fill out?

Moreover, state the deadlines.

Make sure you clearly state the deadlines for the submission of research proposals and for the submission of the complete abstract, full conference paper, journal article, or the chapter. This will help you to get proposals on time, and will help those reading the call for papers to decide whether they can make a submission.

Most importantly, make your call for papers clear and compelling.

As academics are usually very busy, you are likely to receive more proposals if your call for papers gives clear information and has a straightforward submission process. And you might want to mention the importance of the conference or publication somewhere to encourage submissions.

We hope these tips will help you write a successful call for papers. And don't forget to check whether your CFP is clear, concise, and error-free.

(Retrieved from "5 Tips on How to Write a Call for Papers" on Proofed website.)

 Questions:

1. What are the important types of information that need to be included in a call for papers?

2. How can scholars submit their writing proposals for a conference?

3. Why should a successful call for papers have a straightforward submission process?

Passage B

Call for Papers
Chinese Economists Society 2017 North America Conference
March 10–11, 2017
University of Alabama, Tuscaloosa, AL, U.S.A.

The Chinese Economists Society (CES) calls for paper submissions for its 2017 North America Conference, to be held at Tuscaloosa, Alabama, March 10–11 (Friday and Saturday), 2017. The local host for the conference is the University of Alabama, and the conference is co-hosted by Henan University. The theme of the conference is "New Normal of the Chinese Economy: Challenges, Opportunities, and Policy Implications". The conference includes invited keynote speakers, round table forums, and parallel sessions. Arrival and registration of participants will start in the afternoon of March 9. All speeches and sessions will be held on March 10 and 11. Confirmed keynote speakers include:

- Professor Kevin HUANG of Vanderbilt University;
- Professor Yiping HUANG of Peking University;
- Professor Yang YAO of Peking University.

This conference will promote exchanges of academic ideas related to the Chinese economy in a North American venue. It also provides professional opportunities for Ph.D. candidates in North America who do China-related research and/or are interested in China-based employments. This conference will offer a focus-group panel session and other extended activities for these candidates. We encourage Chinese universities to recruit at the conference for new faculty and pursue visiting opportunities in North America for their faculty members. This conference also encourages student participation by offering the best paper award and valuable opportunities for students to network with experienced scholars.

Paper Submissions

CES invites both members and non-members to submit papers and/or to propose organized sessions at the 2017 North America Conference. All fields of specialization within economics will be considered, but papers focusing on the Chinese economy will be given preference. The abstract submission deadline is December 15, 2016.

Unit 1　Calls for Papers and Conference Programs

Individual Presenters

Persons interested in presenting a paper at the conference are asked to submit an abstract of no more than 400 words with title, author name(s), JEL code(s), and keywords via the CES website at http://china-ces.org/Conferences/ConferenceDefault.aspx?ID=45. You will be notified by e-mail by December 31, 2016, as to whether your paper has been accepted for presentation.

Organized Sessions

If you would like to organize one or more sessions on a specific topic and have speakers/presenters lined up, please submit your proposal to Professor Jun MA, CES President, for approval at jma@culverhouse.ua.edu by November 30, 2016. Each organized session should consist of four individual papers. Proposal should contain a tentative name of the session, titles of papers along with their abstracts, as well as names of session presenters and discussants with their e-mails. Please note that papers included in a session must still go through the regular paper submission process through the CES website to be included into the program. Please make reference in the "Comments" section of the form to the organized session (e.g., "This paper is part of a session on urbanization organized by Prof. Wang."). It is the organizer's responsibility to ensure all papers are submitted properly. The submission deadline of individual papers in proposed organized sessions is also December 15, 2016.

Important Dates

November 30, 2016: Organized session proposal submission deadline (submit proposals to jma@culverhouse.ua.edu).

December 15, 2016: Abstract submission deadline for both individual presenters and presenters of proposed organized sessions (submit via the CES website at http://china-ces.org/Conferences/ConferenceDefault.aspx?ID=45).

December 31, 2016: Notification of decision.

Gregory Chow Best Paper Award

We will select an outstanding paper presented at the 2017 CES North America Conference by a junior scholar for the Gregory Chow Best Paper Award. To be eligible for consideration for this prestigious award, the primary author of the paper must be a graduate student or a junior scholar who received his/her Ph.D. within the last five years (no earlier than May 2012). The award winner will receive a certificate and a $1,000 prize. Persons interested in being considered for the award must provide information confirming eligibility at the time of submission. Graduate students' electronic submissions should be followed up by a letter on official university stationary from a professor certifying that the submitter is a graduate student in good standing. An electronic version of this letter should be e-mailed by the professor to the CES President Jun MA at jma@culverhouse.ua.edu by February 12, 2017.

Publications

The CES plans to select a group of high quality papers presented at the conference for special issues for journals such as *China Economic Review*. Papers submitted for consideration of the special issue still need to go through regular review process of the CER. Details about these publication opportunities will be provided later.

Registration

All presenters and conference attendees must register for the conference. Registration should be made online through the conference page at www.china-ces.org under "Conferences". You may wait to register until you find out whether your paper is accepted. Please note that registration fees are non-refundable. All participants must register by February 17 to be included into the final program.

You can join the CES and become a member here: http://www.china-ces.org/AboutCES/Default.aspx?title=Join%20CES. Regular membership is $40 per year while student membership is $15 per year.

Registration Fee Schedule

Before or on January 25, 2017; after January 25, 2017:

- Regular CES member: $80; $120.
- Non-CES member: $125; $180.
- Student CES member: $40; $120.
- Student non-CES member: $60; $180.

Unit 1 Calls for Papers and Conference Programs

Contact Information

- For academic matters: Dr. Jun MA at jma@culverhouse.ua.edu.
- For general inquiries: Dr. Zijun LUO at CES2017NA@gmail.com or luozijun@shsu.edu.

(Retrieved from "Calls for Papers" on Henan University School of Economy website.)

 Questions:

1. How many deadlines are mentioned in the call for papers?
2. What are the requirements for proposal and abstract submission?
3. Who might be the winner of Gregory Chow Best Paper Award?
4. How much is the registration fee for student participants?

Part IV
Reading for Speaking

The following two passages are related to how to build conference programs. Read the passages and discuss in groups to answer the questions.

Passage A

Conference program is the scheme of the conference, and it serves as a guide to the conference activities and may also be named as conference schedule, conference agenda, or conference plan. The agenda of the conference would be a motivating factor for the invitees to decide whether they should consider participating in or ignore the conference. The best way for organizers to have everything under control would be to create a conference agenda which will detail the reasons why the conference is being held.

Here are a couple of tips for creating a conference agenda.

Conducting Pre-event Surveys

Before you come up with a schedule for your conference, you'll need to know what the attendees want to learn. A good way for you to gauge the different kinds of sessions that your conference should hold is to ask for the opinions of your invitees. And what is the better way to ask them than through pre-event surveys?

The simple questions which the survey needs to answer are:

- What do the attendees hope to take away from the conference?
- What kind of sessions will they benefit from the most?
- How do they hope to increase their knowledge in regards to a particular topic?

By answering these simple questions, you will know exactly what needs to be discussed during the conference, which in turn will help you figure out the speakers you can contact to participate in the event.

Offering Exposure to Sponsors

Conference organizers are always thinking of creative ways to provide value for their sponsors. Since the program is always going to be viewed all throughout the conference, the sponsors will see this as a perfect opportunity for them to show their company profile or brands to the attendees. Solutions such as sponsor sessions and sponsored areas are great ways for them to connect directly with the attendees. Having an agenda that is able to provide proper exposure on behalf of your partners is very important if you want to secure your conference sponsors.

Making the Conference Social Media-friendly

If you want people to take interest in your conference or at least hear about it, the simplest thing that you can do is to make sure that you take advantage of social media. Millions of people use social media every day, so it is perfect for you to share whatever information that will interest people and get them to register for your conference. It's a viable marketing strategy and a lot of organizers take the opportunity to use social media as it is one of the easiest and quickest ways to advertise a conference.

Unit 1 Calls for Papers and Conference Programs

Facilitating the Engagement Between the Attendees and the Conference

Make sure that you learn as much as you can in regards to how your conference is going in terms of success. This means that you'll need to come up with a way for your attendees to engage with you as much as possible so that you can acquire the information you need; the easiest way in which you can do so is through social media templates. Make sure that each session can be liked and rated which allows the organizer to collect valuable information and to gain insights as to what the attendees enjoyed or hated. You can also gain this information via survey questionnaires you can hand out after every session. Remember that you will need this information in the future as it will help you know what you can improve to make your next conference a success.

(Retrieved from "12 Tips for Building a Conference Agenda" on Bizzabo website.)

 Questions:

1. Is it necessary for conference organizers to conduct pre-event surveys?

2. How can you secure your conference sponsors in the agenda?

3. Do you agree that using social media is the easiest way to advertise a conference? Why or why not?

Passage B

Usually the scholars invited to a conference expect to know everything about it, so they are provided with as much information as that can be put in the conference program. Here are the information items that should be placed into the conference program.

A Brief Introduction of the Organization

Once you start creating an academic conference program, you should at least have a brief introduction that tells the audience the name of your organization (such as a university), when it was founded, what its smart goals are, and its major achievements. Just remember that you shouldn't go too much into detail as you still have to share other things.

The Speakers

An academic conference is an event where a lot of formal discussions are going to take place. Naturally, a couple of keynote speakers will address certain serious or edge topics towards the audience. So you will have to provide the information about the speakers since they may be the reason for one's deciding to attend the conference.

What you'll have to do first is writing down the complete names of all the keynote speakers. Be sure to include the first name, last name, and middle initial so that they won't be confused for anyone else. Once that's done, you must then provide a brief background of these speakers, and the information regarding what the speakers have achieved, where they graduated from, or just about any other relevant information. And lastly, you'll want to put in when each of them is going to participate in the conference.

The Schedule

Now that you are preparing a conference program that will be looked at constantly by a lot of scholars who are going to attend the conference, you'll need to take into account the number of speakers and the diverse academic activities. In addition, you need to count the number of days that the conference is going to last because most academic conferences usually don't just end in a single day.

Then you may proceed to place the schedule into the program. Just make sure that you put in the type of the discussion or activity into the schedule and also include the complete name of the person who will be holding the session. And lastly, place in the exact time as to when each of the discussions or the activities is going to take place.

Layout of the Area

Since a lot of discussions will be held on the conference and there are certain facilities that participants will need to get to, then all the relevant information must be available on the schedule. This means that you will have to provide all of them with the simple layout of the venue so that they will easily be able to get to wherever they need to be. Be sure that it is a detailed floor plan which points things like the stage setup and where the audience is meant to sit during the discussions.

The Sponsors of the Conference

Unless your organization is the only one handling all the expense tracking, you'll need to provide a description of all the other institutions or people that are sponsoring your conference. You'll have to mention them as they are the ones that provide the funds which allow you to run the conference and not recognizing them might lead to some very big problems in the near future.

In order to avoid any issues, the only thing that you need to do is to mention your sponsors in the "Thank You" section of your program. Be sure to include the logo designs of your sponsors as well as their names to ensure that people know who they are.

Organizing a conference means lots of work and tasks to manage; you'd better follow the tips to develop a well-scheduled conference program.

(Retrieved from "What Should Be in the Conference Program?" on Template website.)

 Questions:

1. Why is it necessary to introduce the keynote speakers in a conference program?

2. How should you schedule a conference?

3. What does the layout of a conference venue look like?

Part V
Reading for Writing

The following is a template to schedule a conference program. Create a conference program related to your research field by using the template.

Day and Date	8:30 9:00	9:00 10:00	10:00 10:30	10:30 12:30	12:30 14:00	14:00 16:30	16:30 17:00
Monday, Dec.13, 2012	Conference registration	Opening ceremony; keynote address	Morning refreshment	Keynote address	Lunch	Parallel session	Coffee break
Tuesday, Dec.14, 2012	Parallel session	Invited speaker; parallel session	Morning refreshment	Parallel session	Lunch	Invited speaker; parallel session	Coffee break; end
Wednesday, Dec.15, 2012	Workshop						

Exercises

I. Read the following conference call for papers and then complete the tasks.

The 4th International Conference on Advanced Research in Education

The 4th International Conference on Advanced Research in Education (EDUCATIONCONF), November 26–28, 2021 in Oxford, U.K., is the premier forum for the presentation of new advances and research results in education theory and practice.

This conference is a **prestigious** event, organized to **provide an international platform** for academicians, researchers, managers, industrial participants, and students to **share their research findings** with global experts. All full paper submissions will be **peer-reviewed** and evaluated based on **originality**, technical and/or research depth, accuracy, and relevance to conference theme and topics.

Conference Theme and Topics

The conference is **seeking submissions** related to the following conference topics: Education Theory and Practice, Education Policy and Administration, Child and Family Education, and Learning. Other related topics will also be considered.

- Education Theory and Practice:
  - Counselor Education
  - Educational Foundations
  - Education Practice Trends and Issues
  - Theory and Practice of Physical Education Development
  - Teaching Materials and Courseware Construction
  - Education and Research Management
  - Educational Measurement and Evaluation
  - Teaching Method Promotion

- Pedagogy
- Curriculum, Research, and Development

• Education Policy and Administration:
- Educational Administration
- Education Policy and Leadership
- Rural Education
- Student Affairs
- Lifelong Education
- Education, Research, and Globalization
- Teacher Education
- Education and Management
- Continuous Education
- Higher Education
- Public Education Policy
- Comparison of Sports Education in Different Cultures
- Sports for Health Education
- Adult and Continuing Education

• Child and Family Education:
- Early Childhood Education
- Teaching Talent Training
- Special Education
- Home Education
- Elementary Education
- Primary Education
- Secondary Education
- Comparison of Child Education in Different Countries

• Learning:
- Lifelong Learning
- E-learning
- Teaching and Learning
- Learning Difficulties
- Learning Psychology

Unit 1 Calls for Papers and Conference Programs

II. Read the following template for a call for papers and a call for papers of ICOAH 2021. Discuss with your partners whether the call for papers suits the template or not.

Template

Name of the conference

Date of the conference

Link to the conference website

It is a pleasure to invite you to <Conference name>. The conference is organized by <Department & organization> and will take place in <Location> on <Conference dates>.

<Brief history on your organization/conference and why recipients should submit>.

The theme of <Conference name> will be <Conference theme>.

Topics of Interest

<List of topics>

Guide for Authors

The deadline to submit abstracts is <Submission deadline>.

To submit your abstract, please click on the following link: <Link to the abstract management system log in page or online form>.

<Insert any relevant information, guidelines, and links>

Important Dates

Deadline for submission: < Deadline for submission>.

Notification of acceptance: <Date of notification of acceptance>.

Deadline for final paper submission: < Deadline for final paper submission>.

Organizing Committee:

<Roles and names of the Organizing Committee>

> For any enquiries regarding the program, please contact: <E-mail address>.
>
> For all general enquiries, please contact: <E-mail address>.
>
> We look forward to seeing you at <Conference name>.
>
> Sincerely,
>
> <Name of the chair>
>
> (Retrieved from "A Call for Papers Template for You to Use" on Ex Ordo website.)

ICOAH 2021—The 8th International Conference on Arts and Humanities 2021

Deadline: May 20, 2021 | **Date:** September 21, 2021–September 22, 2021

Venue/Country: Online Conference, Sri Lanka

Please send us your research abstracts by May 20, 2021. All submissions will be evaluated in a double-blind review process by a committee of internationally recognized scholars. Acceptance notification will be sent by June 3, 2021. Accepted researchers must register by the final registration deadline, July 22, 2021, in order to be present at the conference. Full paper submission deadline (for conference proceedings) will be on October 15, 2021.

Conference Main Tracks

- Interdisciplinary Humanities
- New Technology and Arts
- Art in Society
- Research-creation in Visual and Performing Arts
- Humanities and Social Sciences
- Applied Arts
- Arts Education
- Journalism, Media, and Mass Communications

Publication

All accepted abstracts for the 8th International Conference on Arts and Humanities 2021 (ICOAH 2021) will be published in the conference abstract book

Unit 1 Calls for Papers and Conference Programs

with an associated ISBN.

All full papers sent for conference proceedings will be subjected to a double-blind reviewing process and will be published electronically with an ISSN 2357–2744 in the proceedings with a DOI Number (DOI prefix: 10.17501).

Accepted papers published in conference proceedings will be submitted to Google Scholar, Scopus, and Thomson Reuters for possible indexing.

(Retrieved from "The 8th International Conference on Arts and Humanities 2021" on Fine Arts Conference website.)

III. **Analyze the following calls for papers to better understand the CFP formats in humanities and social sciences and then complete the tasks.**

Sample 1

Depling 2021: 6th International Conference on Dependency Linguistics

When	March 21, 2022–March 25, 2022
Where	Sofia, Bulgaria
Submission Deadline	September 27, 2021
Notification Due	November 10, 2021
Final Version Due	November 30, 2021

Depling 2021 will be held at the SyntaxFest in Sofia, during the week of March 21–March 25, 2022. The event will be held online, face-to-face or hybrid, depending on the health situation. The proceedings will be published preemptively, in December 2021.

Depling is a bi-annual conference dedicated to dependency-based approaches in linguistics and natural language processing (NLP). Dependencies, directed labeled graph structures representing hierarchical relations between morphemes, words, or semantic units, have now become the standard representation of syntactic resources and NLP technologies. Depling has become the central event for people discussing the linguistic significance of these structures, their theoretical and formal foundations, their processing, and their use in NLP tools.

Selected Topics of Interest

For this edition, we would like to put a special emphasis on two topics of interest:

- the epistemological and historical foundations of dependency linguistics (how dependency is defined, how it emerged, how it was formalized, etc.);
- relations between theoretical dependency linguistics and NLP tasks (how, e.g., syntactic models are framed to achieve specific tasks, how the results of such computational tasks modify our conceptions about linguistic modeling, etc.).

Other topics are of course welcome. Topics include but are not limited to:

- the use of dependency structures in theoretical linguistics;
  - the use of syntactic trees to model syntactic relations;
  - the use of semantic, valency-based, or predicate-argument graph structures;
  - the use of dependency-like structures to model semantic and pragmatic phenomena related to information structure;
  - the use of dependency-like structures beyond the sentence (e.g., to model discourse phenomena);
  - the elaboration of formal lexicons for dependency-based syntax and semantics, including descriptions of collocations and paradigmatic relations;
  - the use of dependency in the field of linguistic universals, and typology.
- historical and epistemological foundations of dependency grammar:
  - the definition of the very notion of dependency;
  - the development and the use of dependency-based diagrams;
  - dependency grammar and its relation to other formalisms;
  - the use of dependency-like concepts in the history of grammar and linguistics.
- the use of dependency structures in corpus linguistics:
  - corpus annotation and development of dependency-based treebanks and other linguistic resources of written and spoken texts;
  - recent advances in dependency-based parsing, and text generation;
  - cross-lingual dependency parser evaluation, with particular emphasis on intrinsic evaluation metrics.
- the relation between dependency-based grammar and other fields of science, such as the psycholinguistic relevance of dependency grammar.

Unit 1 Calls for Papers and Conference Programs

Paper Submission Information

Papers should describe original work related to dependency-based linguistics. They should emphasize completed work rather than intended work, and should indicate clearly the state of completion of the reported results. Submissions will be judged on correctness, originality, technical strength, significance, and relevance to the conference, and interest to the attendees. All the details for submission can be found on the conference page.

Important Dates

September 06, 2021: Announcement of conference modality

September 27, 2021: Submission deadlines for long and short papers

November 01, 2021: Review deadlines for long and short papers

November 10, 2021: Acceptance notification

November 30, 2021: Camera-ready version

March 21–25, 2022: Conference

Attendants are encouraged but not obliged to participate in the whole SyntaxFest.

Contact

E-mail: depling2021@depling.org

Website: http://depling.org/depling2021/

(Retrieved from "Depling 2021: 6th International Conference on Dependency Linguistics" on WikiCFP website.)

Sample 2

① *Culture, Theory and Critique* (CTC) invites original full-length article submissions for its upcoming open issues.

② *Culture, Theory and Critique* is an international and interdisciplinary refereed journal for the transformation and development of critical theories in the humanities and social sciences. It aims to critique and reconstruct theories by interfacing them with one another and by relocating them in new sites and conjunctures. The journal's success depends on contributions from a variety of sources, so that debate between different perspectives can be stimulated. One of the aims of the journal is to break down theoretical hierarchies and latent intellectual hegemonies.

③ To this end, every endeavor will be made to incorporate perspectives from diverse cultural, intellectual, and geographical contexts. We therefore particularly encourage work which addresses and contextualizes theories, texts (including cinema, media, fine arts, scientific treatises, etc.) and ethnographic material produced outside of North America and Western Europe. We also encourage submissions of original English translations or introductions/summaries of critical theory works originally published in other languages.

④ *Culture, Theory and Critique* also invites submissions to the journal's Views section. Acknowledging the increasingly diverse ways in which theoretically-informed work in tune with its time is being crafted, and recognizing that not all such work will be appropriate for the normal processes of double-blind peer review, *Culture, Theory and Critique* is now accepting submissions of work to Views that does not conform to the normal original research article format. Submissions may include (but are not restricted to) interviews, field notes, and long-form review essays. Submission length should normally be 3,000~5,000 words. All such submissions must be clearly aligned with CTC's aims and scope, and will be subject to review by the Editorial Board. Please note that such submissions are not double-blind peer reviewed. Authors wishing to submit work of this kind for consideration should not upload their work into the journal's submission portal. In the first instance, authors should contact the Editor-in-Chief (Greg Hainge, Editor-in-Chief, g.hainge@uq.edu.au) with details of their intended submission; only once in principle agreement to consider the piece for publication has been reached, should manuscripts be sent directly to the Editor-in-Chief for review by the Editorial Board.

⑤ Please visit our website (http://www.tandfonline.com/toc/rctc20/current) for instructions and guidelines on how to submit an article.

(Retrieved from "News, Offers, and Calls for Papers" on Taylor & Francis Online website.)

Unit 1 Calls for Papers and Conference Programs

1. Discuss the similarities and differences between a conference call for papers and a journal call for papers.

2. A clear-cut organization with subheadings can help the readers better understand the call for papers. Match each paragraph in Sample 2 with the most appropriate subheadings listed below. Put a slot (/) if no subheading is necessary.

   A. Background Information

   B. Topics of Interest

   C. Deadline

   D. Paper Submission

   E. Contact

   Para. 1 _____   Para. 2 _____   Para. 3 _____

   Para. 4 _____   Para. 5 _____

📖 Project

Work in groups. Collect ten conference calls for papers in two different disciplines of humanities and social sciences. You need to perform the following tasks: identify the themes in the calls for papers; summarize and analyze the structure of the calls for papers; compare the similarities and differences in terms of the requirements of abstract and full paper submission between the two disciplines; and report the group work to the class.

Unit 2

Titles and Abstracts

Part I
Introducing the Unit

As graduate students, we read with clear academic purposes like finding some information before attending a lecture or selecting research articles for a literature review. How can we be sure that some articles serve our purposes while others do not? Read the titles and abstracts of the articles. A title is the starting point of scientific research and an abstract is a highly condensed version of a research paper that highlights the major points covered by the paper. As we all know, the title and the abstract are the most visible parts of a research article. In fact, scholars sometimes just read the title and the abstract because some databases only contain the title, the author list, and the abstract of an article. Learning to read, understand, and identify important information conveyed by the title and the abstract can greatly enhance our reading efficiency and help us to decide whether a research article will be useful for us.

In the following parts, we are going to read, learn, and discuss the features and structures of titles and abstracts from various academic sources, and try to critically evaluate them.

After finishing this unit, you are expected to achieve the following learning objectives:

- to understand the essential components of titles and abstracts;
- to get acquainted with functions fulfilled by different moves of abstracts;
- to use signal phrases in writing different moves of abstracts;
- to be able to comment on the adequacy of titles and abstracts;
- to identify differences among abstracts from different disciplines.

Unit 2 Titles and Abstracts

Part II
Reading for Expressions

Study the bold-faced expressions that are often used in the title or abstract of a research paper.

Expressions in Titles

A. Stating the Nature of the Study

- Mobile **Data-driven** Language Learning: Affordances and Learners' Perception
- **A Mixed-method Study** to Examine the Mental Health Problems of College Students Who Had Left-behind Experience
- **A Meta-analysis**: Vegetarian Diet and Depression Scores
- Implementing Meta-cognitive Learning Strategies to Improve Arabic Comprehension Competences: **An Intervention Study** Among Arabic-speaking Tenth Graders
- Changes in Beverage Purchases Following the Announcement and Implementation of South Africa's Health Promotion Levy: **An Observational Study**

B. Stating the Content of the Study

- **Application of** Precautionary Principle in International Trade Law and International Environmental Law: A Comparative Assessment
- **The Features and Mission of** Sport Psychology in China

Expressions in Abstracts

A. Introducing the Purpose of the Study

- This study **attempts to** determine the effectiveness and efficiency of different learning strategies.
- This study **is intended to** provide a holistic look at the use of arts in an exemplary elementary classroom.
- This study **aims to** systematically review and analyze the available literature on the protection of ancient buildings.
- **It briefly describes** the way fluency is conceptualized in four language tests, as embodied in their respective assessment criteria, **to show** where the field is at present.

- **The present study examined** the relationship between age of acquisition and bilingual development for native Chinese children who learned English as a foreign language.
- This review **presents readers with an overall picture of** what Chinese sport psychologists are doing and what concerns they have in their research and practice.
- **To analyze the potential ways** the threats might unfold in the future, four scenarios of possible terrorism are put forward.

B. Explaining the Research Method

- **A mixed-method** involving a quantitative survey and a qualitative interview **was employed to** explore the influence of the left-behind experience on the mental health of college students.
- **This longitudinal study investigated** the effects of a particular task on an EFL learner's processing of different linguistic items, overall EFL achievement, and foreign language learning attitude.
- **A questionnaire was conducted** in the elementary school for 6th-grade students and the junior high schools for 1st- through 3rd-grade students.

C. Summarizing the Research Findings

- **It was found that the rates** of drug overdose **had risen to unprecedented numbers** and more than half of incarcerated individuals met the criteria for substance use disorder, placing them at high risk.
- **This research found substantial, varied, and context-dependent evidence of** several levers being associated with mitigating poverty.
- **A multitude of cases showing positive outcomes** for poverty mitigation came from community forest management.
- **Findings show that** despite receiving the same classroom input, the students' acquisition of genre knowledge was non-linear.

D. Discussing the Significance of the Findings or the Contribution of the Study

- The present study **contributes to** the validation of the controversial scale.
- **It was suggested that** students' reading interests be strengthened by providing and equipping school libraries.
- **The results indicated** a high correlation between study habits and academic results.

Part III
Reading for Ideas

The following three passages discuss constituents of an effective title, moves of an abstract, and different types of abstracts respectively. Read the passages and answer the questions to understand the main ideas of each passage.

Passage A

The title of a research paper sets the tone for the entire paper. A good title tells readers instantly what you are writing about, grabs their attention, and builds anticipation for further reading. Therefore, the title of your research paper should be descriptive and concise. It must effectively and accurately represent the content of your paper. If someone reads your title and understands what your paper is about, then you have a good title. Here are a few tips that can help you think of an effective title.

The title often includes the concepts and variables studied in your research project. According to Pyrczak & Bruce (1998), if only a small number of variables are studied, the title of your paper should name those variables. For example, if your research studied how race and gender affect respondents' income, your title can be "Race, Gender, and Income". If many variables are studied in your research and they are too many to list in your title, name a broader concept that would include your variables. For example, "A Study of the Relationships Between Students' GPA, Class Attendance, Study Time and Marijuana, Cocaine, and LSD Use" can be changed to "Student School Performance and Substance Use". Also, your title should be concise; if your title is longer than two lines, make it shorter.

If your research makes unique and significant contributions, such as using an innovative research method or studying a unique population, indicate them in your title. For example, if your research involves military spouses' attitudes towards war, specifying "military spouses" in the title may attract readers who are interested in this population. If your research employs an interesting research method, such as participant observations of police behavior, include this in the title so that readers know you applied uncommon methods of data collection. Similarly, you can include your data analysis techniques in your title; for example, if you used structural equation modeling, you can use the title, "A Structural Equation Model for Juvenile Delinquent Behaviors".

(Adapted from *Student Research and Report Writing: From Topic Selection to the Complete Paper* by G. T. Wang & K. Park in 2016.)

 Questions:

1. In what way does the title of a research paper set the tone for the entire paper?
2. What do the authors mainly talk about in this excerpt?
3. Do we need to include all the variables studied in the title?

Passage B

An abstract, as commonly understood, is a description or factual summary of the much longer paper, and is meant to give the reader an exact and concise knowledge of the full article. It contains information on the following aspects of the research that it describes:

- what the author did;
- how the author did it;
- what the author found;
- what the author concluded.

In order to find out how information on all these four aspects of research is put together in a concise manner, let us consider a typical example of an abstract.

"This paper sets out to examine two findings reported in the literature: one, that during the one-word stage a child's word productions are highly phonetically variable; and two, that the one-word stage is qualitatively distinct from subsequent phonological development. The complete set of word forms produced by a child at the one-word stage was collected and analyzed both cross-sectionally (month by month) and longitudinally (looking for changes over time). It was found that the data showed very little variability and that phonological development during the period studied was qualitatively continuous with subsequent development. It is suggested that the phonologically principled development of this child's first words is related to his late onset of speech." (French, 1989: 69–90)

This example seems to answer the four questions by using the following four moves:

- Move 1: Introducing purpose. This move gives a precise indication of the author's intention, thesis, or hypothesis which forms the basis of the research being reported. It may also include the goals or objectives of research or the problem that the author wishes to tackle.
- Move 2: Describing methodology. In this move, the author gives a good indication of the experimental design, including information on the data, procedures, or method(s) used and, if necessary, the scope of the research being reported.
- Move 3: Summarizing results. This is an important aspect of abstracts where the author mentions his observations and findings and suggests solutions to the problem, if any, posed in the first move.
- Move 4: Presenting conclusions. This move is meant to interpret results and draw inferences. It typically includes some indication of the implications and applications of the present findings.

We have all the four moves present as demonstrated respectively by the four sentences of the abstract above: The first sentence introduces the purpose of the research being reported; the next sentence describes methodology, followed by sentence three, which summarizes results; and then the final sentence presents conclusions.

(Adapted from *Analyzing Genre* by V. K. Bhatia in 2013.)

 Questions:

1. What is an abstract?
2. What information should be included in an abstract?
3. What are the four moves of a research paper's abstract?

Passage C

The abstract is the primary "selling feature" of a paper. Apart from the title, it is the section that readers go to in order to determine whether they are interested in looking at the rest of the paper. It is the section of a paper that all scholars who have access to a database can read since full access to complete articles is limited to those with an institutional or personal subscription. Thus, the abstract has a two-fold purpose: to entice readers to read the whole paper and to provide sufficient information for readers to make an informed decision.

Abstracts tend to fall into two types: They report on results, or they summarize. Abstracts that focus on results concentrate on the findings themselves and what can be concluded from them. In contrast, summary abstracts put together the four essential elements from each section of the paper:

- The Introduction section provides the importance of the area of study, the purpose of the study, and perhaps the research questions or hypotheses.
- The Method section provides essential information about how the study was conducted.
- The Results section states what was found. It is typically handled in one of two ways: either the results are "indicated" or provided in a style called "informative". Examples of indicated results are, "The results of the three experiments are presented" or "The data indicated several variables to be pertinent". The actual results of the experiments and the pertinent variables are not stated in the abstract. This use of indicated results seems to be less effective as a selling tool for a paper compared to abstracts that inform the reader of the results. Abstracts that state the key results are especially helpful in determining whether the paper is of value to the reader.
- The Discussion section provides a statement about the contribution of the paper to the field. Some disciplines, such as medicine and experimental psychology, may have other more formalized structures for the abstract. Regardless of the field, it is important to consider that the abstract is the section that a reader sees when searching for scholarly resources. It should be written to emphasize the key importance of the paper based on the study being reported.

(Adapted from *Writing and Publishing Science Research Papers in English: A Global Perspective* by K. Englander in 2013.)

Unit 2 Titles and Abstracts

 Questions:

1. What are the purposes of an abstract?

2. What are the two types of abstracts mentioned in this excerpt?

3. What are the four elements in a summary abstract?

Part IV
Reading for Speaking

The following materials are the titles and abstracts of research papers in different fields. Read the materials and then complete the tasks.

I. Read the title and abstract below and discuss the questions in groups.

Title: Lexical Bundles in Stand-alone Literature Reviews: Sections, Frequencies, and Functions

Abstract: Stand-alone literature reviews exist to synthesize the vast amount of data produced by modern academia, but to date, little research exists on this genre of written academic prose. The present study, therefore, investigates the frequency, dispersion, and discourse functions of lexical bundles in stand-alone literature reviews. A 3.4-million-word corpus of 417 stand-alone literature reviews in psychology, education, and medicine was compiled, and four-word bundles occurring more than 40 times per million words were extracted. Part of the corpus was then divided into IMRD sections, (i.e., introduction, methods, results, and discussion), and the frequency, dispersion, and function of these lexical bundles were examined within each section. Results revealed that lexical bundles in stand-alone literature reviews were identical to those found in other studies of academic writing, which suggests that a core set of bundles for written academic prose may exist. However, the frequency of each bundle differed by section, and concordance lines presented a range of discourse functions. Bundles established research gaps, clarified results and methods, reported data, undergirded interpretations, and contextualized findings. Further research into lexical bundle frequency and use patterns within sections of stand-alone literature reviews is needed to establish pedagogical guidelines for lexical bundle use.

(Adapted from "Lexical Bundles in Stand-alone Literature Reviews: Sections, Frequencies, and Functions" by R. Wright in *English for Specific Purposes*, Vol. 54, 2019.)

 Questions:

1. Do you think the title effectively and accurately represents the content of the paper?
2. Can you predict what concepts and variables are studied in this research project?
3. How is the abstract organized?
4. Can you identify the four moves (introduction, methodology, results, and discussion) of the abstract?

II. Read the following three abstracts and discuss the questions in groups.

Abstract 1

This study aims to investigate the book reading habits and media literacy of students at the faculty of education, in terms of different variables. In this context, we carried out research to see whether there is a relation between the book reading habits and media literacy of students and their departments, grades, habits of using social media, academic grade point averages, and educational background of their parents. In addition, we scrutinized the correlation between their reading habits and media literacy and to what extent these variables account for each other. The results were obtained by using the "Attitude Scale Towards Reading Habit" developed by Gömleksiz (2004) and the "Media Literacy Scale" developed by Korkmaz and Yeşil (2011). According to the results of this study, the attitudes of female students towards reading are higher than those of male students. While there is a positive correlation between reading habits, grade point averages, and media literacy, there is a negative correlation between reading habits and social media using habits. We could not notice any relation between the reading habits of students and the educational background of their parents. Likewise, there was not any relation between the social media using habits of students and the educational background of their parents, whereas there was a low-level correlation between their media literacy and grade point averages.

(Adapted from "Research on Book Reading Habits and Media Literacy of Students at the Faculty of Education" by A. Karadeniz & C. Remzi in *Social and Behavioral Sciences, 174*(1), 2015.)

Abstract 2

This study empirically examines impacts of subject-specific competencies and reading habits on university graduates' income in Japan. Business and economics graduates during 1996 and 2016 at a research university in Tokyo were surveyed. Path analyses of 677 valid responses from graduates employed in the private sector indicated positive impacts of subject-specific competencies and reading habits on income after graduation, as they are recognized as important to respondents' careers. Thus, when reading habits and subject-specific competencies were relevant to the respondents' careers, they indirectly and positively influenced income. No gender differences were noted in business; sufficient observations were not obtained for economics.

(Adapted from "The Impact of Subject-specific Competencies and Reading Habits on the Income of Japanese Business and Economics Graduates" by M. Kato & N. Akinobu in *International Journal of Educational Development, 81*(1), 2021.)

Abstract 3

The Chinese people have great regard for those who read widely, yet little is known about the extracurricular reading behaviors of Chinese students. This study drew on data from two national surveys to investigate the amount of time Taiwanese college students spend on extracurricular reading. Findings are interpreted in relation to prior research on the reading habits of college students internationally. The study found that: (1) female students on average did not spend more time on extracurricular reading than males; (2) students from public institutions, who generally have higher academic competence, did not spend more time reading than students from private institutions; (3) education majors spent the least time on extracurricular reading; (4) newspapers, magazines, and bestsellers were the most popular reading materials, but manga (graphic novels) had medium popularity; and (5) cross-cultural differences might have an impact on the amount of time spent reading and on reading interests.

(Adapted from "Extracurricular Reading Habits of College Students in Taiwan" by S. Chen in *Journal of Adolescent & Adult Literacy*, 50(8), 2007.)

 Questions:

1. Of the three abstracts above, which one(s) is/are result abstract(s) and which one(s) is/are summary abstract(s)?

2. What similarities can you find among the three abstracts in terms of moves?

3. What differences can you find among the three abstracts?

Unit 2 Titles and Abstracts

Part V
Reading for Writing

Based on what you have learned from the reading materials in Part III and Part IV, complete the following two writing tasks related to titles and abstracts.

I. Read Passage A in Part III again and complete the following chart by narrowing down the subjects into titles for research projects.

Subjects	Titles
Education	Does College Education Prepare Students to Obtain a Well-paid Job?
Animal rights	
English	
Entertainment	
Health	
Intelligence	
Sports	

II. Read the three abstracts in the second section of Part IV again and learn the techniques and guidelines for abstract writing. Assume you have done research on extracurricular reading behaviors among your peer students in this digital age. Write an abstract of your own. Your abstract (either results or summary) should be based on your research containing questions on students' reading time, attitudes, purposes, and habits.

Exercises

I. **Comment on the adequacy of each of the following titles for research articles.**

(1) Nurses Report Higher Levels of Job Satisfaction When They Are Permitted to Participate in Decision-making

(2) Effective Communication Between Teachers and School Administrators

(3) The Political Scientist

(4) Are Age and Tenure Related to the Job Satisfaction of Social Workers?

(5) Can Economists Predict Recessions?

(6) The Effects of Peer Coaching on Achievement in English, Mathematics, History, Foreign Language, Geography, and Physics Among Tenth-, Eleventh-, and Twelfth-Graders: An Experiment Conducted in Five Major Urban Areas During the 2001–2002 School Year Using Multiple Measures of Achievement with Analyses by Gender and Grade Level

(7) Forbidden Fruit Tastes Especially Sweet: A Study of Lawyers' Ethical Behavior

(8) The Out-migration from Southern China Is Driven by High Housing Costs

II. **Answer the following questions based on what you have read in Part III.**

(1) When should the title mention only the types of variables studied?

(2) Do the titles of journal articles tend to be longer than the titles of theses and dissertations?

(3) Why should the title of an empirical research paper not state the results of a study?

(4) Which are more formal as titles, statements or questions?

Unit 2 Titles and Abstracts

III. Read the following two titles and abstracts taken from students' research papers and improve them in terms of wording, style, and structure.

Sample 1

Title: Assessment of Knowledge, Attitudes, and Perceptions Regarding Body Donation Among College Students at Nanjing University

Abstract: This semester is my first time to learn anatomy and get to do experiments on a cadaver. And our teacher said that the dead bodies are not enough for future use, which worries him a lot. Body donation can be divided into two categories: One is to donate the whole body to medical schools, and the other is to donate a part of the body to other people in need. The former one is what I am going to do research on. In Chinese culture, body donation is an old taboo. Even though more and more people know burning the body after death would mean nothing but a pile of ash, letting themselves or their beloved ones lie in formaldehyde solution for years and be cut maybe carelessly by medical students is still difficult to accept. The mindset of the middle-aged and the elderly may be hard to change, but to change the condition of body donation in the future relies on the youth. So, it's essential to figure out their attitudes towards body donation to find a solution in the future. As a result, I decide to hand out questionnaires to my classmates in Nanjing University, both students of the Medicine School and those of other majors. In the questionnaire, their gender, age, major, hometown, ethnic, and religion will be taken into consideration, because these factors would possibly affect their mindset. For the first part, I will ask about their knowledge and their acceptance of body donation, whether they are willing to donate their body and the reason. For the second part, I want to know their thoughts on the social condition of body donation and what they think has led to the current condition. For the final part, they must give their solution of how to encourage people to donate their bodies. According to what I get from the questionnaire, I find that not many students know the importance of body donation and human body dissection. Therefore, only a small percentage of students are willing to donate their bodies. Finally, I would conclude the methods of pushing forward body donation supported by the students and come up with some overall solutions to change the current situation of body donation. My aim through this research is to find a way to change the current situation and make anatomy and body dissection more acknowledged and accepted.

Sample 2

Title: An Investigation into the Relationship Between L2 Reading Motivation and Reading Achievement

Abstract: This study aims to study the relationship between learners' motivation towards reading in a foreign language and their reading achievement on a chosen reading task. For this purpose, freshman students enrolled in Department of English of a major university in China took part in the study. Data was collected through a scale on foreign language reading attitudes and motivation, and a reading comprehension test. The data gathered through these two instruments is subjected to statistical analyses. Based on these analyses, the question as to the types of reading motivation dominantly favored by the learners, as well as whether there was a significant relationship between students' motivation and attitudes towards reading in English and their reading achievement are answered. The statistical analysis identified a significant correlation between students' reading motivation scores and reading achievement scores. The result confirms that student motivation enables the students to put more effort on reading; hence it is a key factor in successful reading.

IV. Read the following abstract and then complete the tasks.

Abstract: Magazines, often published periodically with a variety of contents, **have long been successful** in **catering to** magazine readers' various content needs and reading interests. In recent years, interactive digital magazines instead of replicas of printed magazines, based on digital devices, **have been gaining popularity** and preference **due to** their unrivaled convenience and interactivity. **To some extent**, many people's magazine-reading habits have been changed due to their adoption of mobile digital devices. This study **is designed to** analyze mobile digital devices' influence on magazine reading habits amongst university students in Hong Kong. Issues such as mobile digital devices' level of adoption amongst university students and their preferences on devices for different magazine types are analyzed. **Our findings show** that university students in Hong Kong read more types of magazines after they started to use mobile digital devices, mainly using tablets. The findings

Unit 2 Titles and Abstracts

> of the study **are useful for** librarians (academic librarians in particular) and digital publishing vendors to explore the issues concerning services and collection development of interactive digital resources.
>
> (Adapted from "Why Read It on Your Mobile Device? Change in Reading Habit of Electronic Magazines for University Students" by P. Wang et al. in *The Journal of Academic Librarianship, 42*(6), 2016.)

1. **Fill in the blanks with the bold-faced expressions in the text above. Change the form where necessary.**

    (1) This method has been shown _____ for social studies.

    (2) Their knowledge of local language _____ the data collection process.

    (3) Special schools are opened across urban districts to _____ special needs.

    (4) In Iowa alone, up to 500,000 acres of land were farmed in 2008 _____ the increased market value of corn.

    (5) This wellness trend _____ because healthcare systems have adapted virtual arrangements to meet people where they are.

    (6) Characters in fictional and dramatic works are often conventionalized _____.

    (7) The lesson _____ engage students and make them active participants in it.

    (8) _____ that learning attitudes are positively related to learning outcome.

2. **Answer the following questions.**

    (1) What is the research background?

    (2) What is the research target mentioned in this abstract?

    (3) What do the research findings show?

    (4) How can the research findings of this study be useful?

V. Read the following abstract excerpted from a journal article. Pay attention to the bold-faced expressions, and analyze the text to understand the function and structure of a typical abstract in an academic article. Match each paragraph with the most appropriate description below.

① Reading is **the gateway to** success in education. It is the heartbeat of all courses offered in institutions. It is therefore **crucial** to investigate students' reading habits in Colleges of Education and how to **improve the skill**.

② The study was **a descriptive survey** with **a validated questionnaire** on "Reading Habits Among Colleges of Education Students in the Information Age" (RHCESIA). A total number of two hundred students were used from the two Colleges of Education in Oyo town, with gender and age as the moderating variables.

③ The **findings showed** that almost all the respondents understand the importance of reading. 65.5% love to read from their various fields of specialization **on a daily basis** while 25.0% love reading from their **fields of specialization** every week.

④ The study **confirmed** that good reading habits **enhance academic performance**. The study **recommended** that **courses on communication skills** should be included for the first-year students and prose work and fiction such as novels should be a **compulsory** course for second-year students.

(Adapted from "A Survey on the Reading Habits Among Colleges of Education Students in the Information Age" by O. Fatiloro et al. in *Journal of Education and Practice*, 8(8), 2017.)

A. Summarizing results (what the authors found)

B. Presenting conclusions (what the authors concluded)

C. Introducing purposes (what the authors did)

D. Describing methodology (how the authors did it)

Para. 1 _____   Para. 2 _____

Para. 3 _____   Para. 4 _____

Project

Work in groups. Collect ten titles and abstracts from the journal articles in two different disciplines of humanities and social sciences. You need to perform the following tasks: critically analyze the adequacy of each of the titles; identify different moves in the abstracts; summarize and analyze the adequacy of each of the abstracts; compare whether there are differences in terms of moves contained in the abstracts in the two different disciplines; and finally report the group work in class.

Unit 3

Introductions

Part I
Introducing the Unit

In this unit, we are going to learn how to read introductions in research articles. Introduction is the first main section of a research paper with a clear function to set the tone for the reader by giving some idea of the research content as well as the stance of the writer. Being placed at the beginning of a paper, an introduction can include key information like what the research topic is, background of the research, how the writer came to research the topic, and how significant the topic is. It also suggests how the paper is organized. An introduction of a research paper can be as short as a paragraph and as long as several paragraphs, depending on the length and complexity of the writing.

In the following parts, we will read some excerpts from articles published on academic journals to reveal the general purpose, content, and organization of an introduction. Moreover, we will critically assess and discuss the adequacy of some sample introductions from different research materials.

After finishing this unit, you are expected to achieve the following learning objectives:

- to understand the essential components of introductions;
- to identify different moves of introductions;
- to be acquainted with functions fulfilled by different moves of introductions;
- to be able to comment on the adequacy of introductions;
- to become aware of differences among introductions from different disciplines.

Unit 3 Introductions

Part II
Reading for Expressions

Study the bold-faced expressions that are often used in the Introduction section of a research paper.

A. Stating the Purpose of the Current Research

- This paper **argues that** various linguistic domains are susceptible to this hypothesis to a different degree.
- **The purpose of this investigation is** to explore the relationship between these two factors.
- This present study **is undertaken to describe** the college students' extracurricular reading habits and activities.

B. Establishing the Importance of the Research Topic

- Understanding populism and neo-populism **is fundamental to** understanding how democracy works in this region.
- Phonological awareness skills can **play an important/vital role in** the development of decoding abilities in typical readers.
- The onset age of acquisition **becomes an important issue** that may concern parents and education authorities especially for learning a second language.
- Hence the measurement of fluency **is of great interest** to scholars in language testing.
- Understanding what underlies Native American's positive attitude towards alcohol **is essential for** effective intervention.
- The identity of author, Chaucer, **is central to** the understanding of the metaphors.

C. Identifying a Research Gap in the Field of Study

- Indeed, these three models **have largely gone unnoticed up to this point**.
- However, **very little is known** about the effects of demographic tendency on social movement.
- Although it became accepted that mental health might be an important factor, **no systematic analyses** of how important it was in the overall picture of psychoanalysis were carried out.
- To date, **there are few studies that have investigated** the association

between these two factors.

- Short-term studies such as these **do not necessarily show subtle changes** over time.
- The nature of this social phenomenon **remains unclear**.
- To date, the problem **has received scant attention** in the research literature.

D. Establishing the Significance of the Topic as a Problem to Be Addressed

- These observations point to the proposition that **there is a need to increase** research knowledge of community social practices.
- The study of thesis writing at postgraduate level is **an increasingly important area** in applied linguistics.
- The influence of parental psychological functioning and child development **has received considerable critical attention**.

E. Identifying a Controversy Within the Field of Study

- The relationship between democracy and justice **has become a much-debated issue**.
- The nature of creativity is highly subjective, and **there is little agreement** among researchers as to a specific definition.
- **Debate continues about** the best strategies for the management of higher learning institutions.
- More recently, **literature has emerged that offers contradictory findings** about the impact of immigration.
- Onset age of foreign language instruction **has been a controversial and much disputed subject** within the field of second language acquisition in China.

F. Referring to Previous Research to Establish What Is Already Known

- **A considerable amount of literature has been published** on these three models.
- One major theoretical issue that **has dominated the field** for many years concerns the relationship between language and cognition.
- However, **much of the research up to now** has been only descriptive in nature.

G. Describing the Research Design and the Methods Used

- The study **was conducted in the form of a survey**, with data being gathered

via a questionnaire.
- **A combination of quantitative and qualitative approaches was used** in the data analysis of the present research.

Part III
Reading for Ideas

The following two passages discuss the four essential elements and the typical structure of an introduction respectively. Read the passages and answer the questions to understand the main ideas of each passage.

Passage A

Make your introduction succinct and to the point, but include these four items.

First, write an explicit topic statement. Introducing your readers to the problem or issue you are about to investigate is the most important mission of your introduction. Background knowledge may include a brief history of how the issue has developed, or the extent to which the issue has affected or has been important to society. Basic statistics may help to establish that your topic is worthy of investigating. For example, if you are researching adolescent substance use because you believe it seriously affects school performance, give your readers the percentage of adolescents using substances, what substances they use, and how serious the problem is for the society. You might include the percentage of adolescents whose school performance has been affected by their substance use and how serious the impact has been. You can emphasize the significance of your topic by discussing the inadequacy of readers' understanding of the issue and the need for your study.

Second, if your topic statement includes theoretical concepts, you need to provide clear and specific definitions of these concepts in the introduction. It is a good idea to draw upon the definitions researchers use in their published work. For example, if you wish to use the terms "intrinsic work value" and "extrinsic work value", the meaning of these terms may not be self-explanatory to your readers, or there may be multiple definitions scholars have used for these terms. Wang (1996) defined intrinsic work values as the primarily psychological needs that employees desire and seek directly from their work activity. Extrinsic work values are the physiological and social needs that employees desire and seek from their work organization and working context. If this is the way you want to use these terms in your introduction, you should state them upfront so that you will establish a common ground for understanding your research. Similarly, if you are conducting deductive research and would like to start with a theory, you should briefly explain the theory even if you assume many of your readers already know it. After establishing a common understanding of the terms and theories, you may discuss why it is necessary and appropriate for you to test the theory with your research project.

Third, inform your readers of the objectives or purposes of your research, and tell them what you expect to find out from your research. Do you intend to provide some descriptive data on a social issue or a phenomenon? Are you testing the relationship between two variables, or testing a theory? Are you investigating a new issue which has not been studied by other scholars? Or, are you planning to evaluate the effectiveness of an intervention program? Use the introduction to communicate what you want to achieve in the research project. Do you have two objectives for your proposed research? List them both.

Fourth, explicitly state the significance of your research. Tell your readers why the proposed research is worth doing and explain its social or academic significance. For example, if your research project may increase readers' understanding of an important social problem or a timely policy issue, state it in the introduction. If your research project will have a great social applicability, let readers know that your research project may help a great number of people.

(Adapted from *Student Research and Report Writing*: *Form Topic Selection to the Complete Paper* by G. Wang & K. Park in 2016.)

 Questions:

1. What do the authors mainly talk about in this excerpt?

2. What are the four different elements that should be included in the introduction?

3. How can you prove that the topic is worth investigating?

Unit 3 Introductions

Passage B

The Introduction section has a typical structure in English-language research papers. Briefly, based on the research of John Swales (1990, 2004), there are three "moves" or elements that serve to create an intellectual space for the research paper. Move 1 establishes the research territory, including reviewing the existing research which may be insufficient or misguided in dealing with a particular scientific phenomenon. Move 2 establishes a niche or a gap in the literature. Move 3 fills that gap by stating the objective or purpose of the current study. Of course, not every paper will neatly perform the three moves and present them in a sequential fashion, but the vast majority do.

To sum up, the organizational structure of the introduction can be said to move from a general overview of the research terrain to the issues under investigation through three key moves which capture the communicative purposes of the introduction (Swales & Feak, 1994):

- to establish a research territory;
- to identify a niche or a gap in the territory;
- to signal how the topic in question occupies that niche.

In Move 1—establishing a research territory—the writer typically begins to carve out his/her own research space by indicating that the general area is in some way significant. This is often done through reviewing previous research in the field. In addition, the writer may choose to provide background information on the topic being investigated and may define key terms which are essential for the study.

Move 2—establishing a niche—points to a "gap" in the previous research which the research will "fill". For Swales & Feak (1994), the metaphor of the niche or research space is based on the idea of competition in ecology—academic writers seeking to publish must compete for "light and space" as do plants and animals. In Move 2 of the framework, the writer typically establishes a niche by indicating a gap in the previous research or possibly extending a current research approach into a new area. It is through the review of prior research that the gap is established.

In Move 3—occupying the niche—the writer, by outlining the purposes of the research, indicates to the reader how the proposed research will "fill" the identified niche or gap. Sometimes the principal findings will frequently be previewed and theoretical positions as well as methods used may be outlined. It is here that the writer can signal the value or significance of the research. Besides, the overall structure of the article is sometimes previewed. However, this is not considered obligatory.

(Adapted from *Thesis and Dissertation Writing in a Second Language* by B. Paltridge & S. Starfield in 2007; *Writing and Publishing Science Research Papers in English: A Global Perspective* by K. Englander in 2014.)

 Questions:

1. What are the three moves of the introduction?

2. What is the major purpose of each of the three moves?

3. In which part of the introduction can you find the objective or purpose of the current study?

Part IV
Reading for Speaking

The following two passages are the introductions of two research papers in different fields. Read the passages and discuss the questions in groups to understand the content, wording, style, and structure of each introduction.

Passage A

The growth of English medium instruction (EMI) is an increasingly prominent trend in higher education globally. In China, EMI programs have received substantial support from national policies since the turn of the century (Ministry of Education, 2001, 2007a, 2007b; State Council, 2010), and are positioned as an important component of the internationalization of Chinese higher education (Hu et al., 2014). The provision of EMI has thus expanded rapidly in universities in Chinese mainland—by 2006, 132 out of 135 universities that Wu et al. (2010) surveyed had run EMI courses with an average of 44 EMI courses per each university.

Unit 3 Introductions

Despite the growth of EMI programs in China, many studies have revealed observable difficulties that students encounter in listening to English medium lectures (Hu et al., 2014; Hua, 2020), particularly during the transition year when students shift from first language (L1)—taught secondary schools to EMI university programs (Evans & Morrison, 2011, 2016). To overcome such difficulties, it seems highly likely that students need to become more self-regulated and strategic in their learning when adapting to an EMI university environment (e.g., Ding & Stapleton, 2016, in Hong Kong, China; Evans & Morrison, 2011, 2016, in Hong Kong, China; Macaro et al., 2019, in Italy; Soruç & Griffiths, 2018, in Turkey). However, few studies have examined the self-regulated learning of students in EMI programs in contexts such as China, where students need to rapidly adapt to both a new medium of instruction, and to a new educational context, where topic-based lessons are delivered by university teachers.

The present study fills this gap by exploring how first-year students self-regulate their listening, an important yet challenging aspect for Chinese students (Hu et al., 2014), at an EMI transnational university in Chinese mainland. The study explores the self-regulatory listening strategies and processes reported by students while also considering listening proficiency (Goh & Hu, 2014; Vandergrift et al., 2006) and self-efficacy (Graham & Macaro, 2008) to explore the role of these factors in interacting with self-regulatory listening processes.

(Adapted from "Self-regulated Listening of Students at Transition from High School to an English Medium Instruction Transnational University in China" by S. Zhou & H. Rose in *System*, Vol. 103, 2021.)

 Questions:

1. What is the role of this introduction in relation to the whole research paper?
2. How is the introduction organized?
3. How does the introduction establish a research territory?
4. What is the gap or niche in the previous research?
5. How can the present research fill in the gap?

Passage B

Over the past several decades, plagiarism research has acquired a great deal of attention. Plagiarism policy has been rightfully spotlighted by several studies, as plagiarism policy is the document upon which students, professors, and other faculty should depend for educational information about plagiarism as well as guidance regarding their institution's stance for mediating cases of alleged plagiarism. Yet analyses have revealed that policy frames plagiarism as a transgressive act (Adam et al., 2017; Hu & Sun, 2017; Sutherland-Smith, 2011) by situating it alongside other moral breaches in academia (e.g., cheating, copying).

These studies have investigated plagiarism policy in a rich variety of cross-institutional and transnational contexts. Despite nearly universal agreement that plagiarism policies raise more questions than they answer and are thus in need of an educative approach, one facet lacking from these studies is the consideration of students who potentially face the obstacle of navigating multiple plagiarism policies simultaneously. Some institutions of higher education in Europe and Asia, for instance, have been shown to possess multiple plagiarism policies at the same institution (Ronai, 2020). In the U.S., though it is more the norm than the exception for U.S. universities to have centralized plagiarism policies, the possibility of multiple plagiarism policies existing at the same institution is of particular importance for the university students themselves, as discipline-specific plagiarism policies may dictate procedures and regulations more so than an institution's centralized policy (McGrail & McGrail, 2015).

The purpose of this study was to address this gap in the literature by examining the plagiarism policies of nine of the colleges at the University of Iowa, a public university at which nearly 24,000 undergraduates are enrolled. The significance of this study stems from the need to consider the reality of many of these undergraduate students, who—by enrolling in core coursework across several disciplines—must by extension potentially negotiate the individual plagiarism policies of the colleges in which these disciplines are housed. In addition, because it is common for students to work towards the completion of their core coursework as first- and second-year students, their knowledge and skills of academic writing in general and discipline-specific expectations specifically are still developing, thus rendering their understanding of these policies critical.

(Adapted from "Collage of Confusion: An Analysis of One University's Multiple Plagiarism Policies" by W. Merkel in *System*, Vol. 96, 2021.)

 Questions:

1. Do you think this excerpt is in accordance with the typical structure of the introduction provided in Passage B in Part III?

2. Is the introduction written in a cohesive way?

3. What is the research purpose of the present study? How can the study fill in the research gap?

Part V
Reading for Writing

Read Passage A and Passage B in Part IV again. Based on what you have learned from Part III, write a brief summary for each passage with no less than 200 words to answer the following questions.

- What does "research territory" mean?
- What is the research gap?
- How does the research fill in the research gap?

Exercises

I. Read the following paragraph written by a student and decide whether it is successful to indicate the importance of the research topic ("The Prevalence of Depression Among Adolescents"). Give your reasons.

> In the new millennium, the public are increasingly aware of the importance of the psychological well-being of all citizens. Because of this recognition by the public, it is important to conduct more studies that shed light on the prevalence of well-being, starting with the psychological well-being of adolescents, who will soon be adults.

II. Read the following introductions taken from students' research papers and improve them in terms of wording, style, and structure.

Introduction 1

> Feral cats live outdoors; they are unowned and avoid contact with people. They can breed for dozens of generations and become aggressive local top predators. So far, my living environment has mainly been the university campus and I have been observing a lot of feral cats nearby. Those cats are very popular, but their rising popularity is causing some problems to the campus, such as damaging the public facilities, making disturbing noises, spreading viruses, and so on. Research has even already proved that increased densities of feral cats have potentially negative effects on wildlife populations (Lowe et al., 2000). Obviously, their popularity needs to be controlled and managed in order to guarantee the sustainable development of university campuses. Some people think the most effective solution to dealing with the excess feral cats is to catch and kill them all. That's also what the public mainly think of when coming to this problem. However, research needs to be done into the "management" of feral cats to see whether blindly killing is the most effective choice or not. Literature indicates that totally wiping out feral cats from university

Unit 3   Introductions

campuses is not a wise decision because killing the cats all is an unpractical approach. Aiming to provide approaches to remedy the current gap from blindly killing to rational control, this present research explores the most efficient and effective management program which can be applied by Chinese universities to achieve feral cat control.

Introduction 2

Have safe and affordable housing for women and families experiencing homelessness and domestic violence was a social policy issue in China. Increasingly the focus of research and policy work is on women and family access to safe and affordable housing. Scholarly research over recent decades said that domestic violence is often a precedent to an individual or a family's pathway to homelessness (Johnson et al., 2008; Spinney, 2012). Research also identified that lack of access to appropriate, secure, and affordable housing are reasons for women to remain in situations where they continue to experience domestic violence (Burnett, 2016; Cripps & Habibis, 2019). The conditions of local housing markets are critical to addressing women's and family homelessness in China.

III. Read the following introduction and then complete the tasks.

This article considers the construct of fluency. While laypeople use the word as a synonym for overall oral proficiency, in the field of second language assessment **it is seen as** one component of oral proficiency, **complemented by** others, such as the accuracy and complexity of the linguistic forms that speakers use. Lennon (1990) has termed these two definitions as the broad and narrow sense of fluency, respectively. The narrow sense has also been defined in different ways.

The discrepancies between these definitions come from the viewpoint taken: Lennon (1990) **takes the viewpoint of** the listener, whereas Fillmore (1979) and Lennon (2000) describe the viewpoint of the speaker (with the speaker's actual ease or trouble in speech production processes). Segalowitz (2010, p.165) captures these viewpoints, **distinguishing between** cognitive fluency—"the efficiency of operation of the underlying processes responsible for the production of utterances"—and perceived fluency—"the inferences listeners make about speakers' cognitive fluency based on their perceptions". Similarly, Luoma (2004, p.88) also acknowledges the different viewpoints when describing the temporal characteristics of fluency; the characteristics "[...] are not simply descriptions of a speaker's speech but also of a listener's perception of it".

In this article I consider how second language assessment practice might **be informed by** considering research on fluency in other areas of applied linguistics. First, I briefly review how fluency is described and reflected in the assessment criteria of four current tests, to show where the field is at present. I then review the research on fluency in different disciplines—applied linguistics, psycholinguistics, conversation analysis, and sociolinguistics—and sketch out each discipline's implications for language testing practice. Because space limitations make it impossible to be exhaustive, most of the review will be on "applied linguistics", a term used for studies from the field of second language acquisition that have **potential applications** for language testing in mind. Hopefully, by focusing on such studies, combined with those from the other fields, the review will **provide** language testers **new insights into** the assessment of fluency.

(Adapted from "Fluency in Second Language Testing: Insights from Different Disciplines" by N. H. Jong in *Language Assessment Quarterly, 15*(3), 2018.)

1. **Fill in the blanks with the bold-faced expressions in the text above. Change the form where necessary.**

    (1) The findings also _____ this research area.

    (2) Previous research findings have offered _____ the development of students' academic performance.

    (3) _____ a breakthrough in alleviation of poverty in India.

    (4) If deemed appropriate, that examination is _____ a further analysis carried out by external experts.

    (5) _____ the different regions can often be traced back to cultural or historical factors.

    (6) The students sometimes have difficulty _____ Spanish and Portuguese.

Unit 3　Introductions

　　(7) _____ filial duty, we should always follow our parents' opinions.

　　(8) These policy decisions certainly need to _____ research.

2. **Answer the following questions.**

　　(1) What is the research territory established in this introduction?

　　(2) What is the gap mentioned in this introduction?

　　(3) What is the researcher going to do in order to fill in the research gap?

　　(4) Is the use of the first person (e.g., "I" and "we") acceptable in the introduction of a research paper? Give your reasons.

IV. **Read the following introduction excerpted from a journal article. Pay attention to the bold-faced expressions, and analyze the text to understand the function and structure of a typical introduction in an academic article. Match each paragraph with the most appropriate description below.**

> ① Undergraduate research (UR) **is a growing movement** in higher education. It is embraced at all types of institutions and is increasingly prevalent across the humanities, social sciences, and sciences. While it has been virtually omnipresent in the sciences for decades, UR in economics **is still in its infancy**.
>
> ② A recent survey by McGoldrick (2008a) indicates that only a small fraction of economics departments considers UR an important goal for their undergraduate program. In fact, only 36% of programs surveyed reported "the ability to make an original contribution to the discipline" to be an important goal of their senior capstone experience.
>
> ③ While the case for UR has been articulated in other disciplines, economists by and large **have yet to recognize the value** of investing time and energy on UR in any kind of comprehensive way.
>
> ④ In this paper, we argue for the implementation of numerous types of UR that can benefit all economics students, not just those bound for graduate school.
>
> ⑤ Fundamentally, UR helps students learn how knowledge is constructed in a discipline by offering them firsthand experience with the process. In this sense, UR can be thought of as an overarching pedagogical approach that individual faculty and entire

departments can implement to better teach students the "economic way of thinking".

⑥ Even if one understands the potential value of UR in economics, it can be challenging to build a successful UR program. Casual empiricism suggests that many economists may be hesitant to get involved in UR because they do not know when to get students involved or where it is most appropriate to incorporate it into the curricula. For example, it is one thing to know that a research-based service-learning project is considered UR, but it is another to know when the project is going to work best. **Moreover,** what skills can students learn in such an experience that can be built on in subsequent UR experiences? We argue that quality UR requires more than good mentoring by a single passionate faculty member. It requires a department committed to the kinds of curricular development that provide students with the opportunity to build foundational skills in their earlier years. **The purpose of this paper is to** provide a roadmap for the faculty and departments to use in implementing meaningful UR experiences across the board.

⑦ In the process, **the paper makes several contributions to** economists' understanding of UR. First, we develop a taxonomy of the various ways in which undergraduate economics majors can engage in meaningful research that develops critical thinking skills. These include: 1) course-based activities (e.g., shorter quantitative writing assignments, naturalistic observation, etc.); 2) course-based projects (e.g., semester-long service-learning projects, term papers in econometrics, etc.); 3) capstone experiences (e.g., honors theses, senior seminar papers); and 4) collaborative research with faculty. Second, because the existence of multiple forms of UR is ultimately suggestive of a hierarchy based on knowledge, complexity, and student independence, we create a developmental model of UR to guide the creation of new programs and improvement of existing ones. This includes the articulation of appropriate learning goals at each level of UR, including theoretical and methodological content, critical thinking, and research skills.

⑧ The paper **proceeds as follows**: 1) In Section II we define exactly what we mean by undergraduate research and show how the steps of the research process can be directly linked to Hansen's (2006) list of proficiency that all economics students should acquire as undergraduates; 2) in Section III, we develop our taxonomy of the basic types of research experiences and relate them to well-defined learning goals and objectives. We also detail many of the key characteristics of each activity that faculties need to consider when making pedagogical decisions; 3) in Section IV we conclude with a discussion of six concrete recommendations for departments designing new programs or improving existing ones.

(Adapted from "Creating Quality Undergraduate Research Programs in Economics: How, When, Where (and Why)" by S. B. DeLoach et al. in *The American Economist, 57*(1), 2012.)

A. Importance of the research topic

B. Pointing out the people who are affected by the problem researched

C. Background information

D. Describing the research area

E. Contribution of the current study

F. Organization of the paper

G. Pointing out the research gap

H. Research purpose

Para. 1 _____   Para. 2 _____   Para. 3 _____   Para. 4 _____

Para. 5 _____   Para. 6 _____   Para. 7 _____   Para. 8 _____

Project

Work in groups. Collect ten introductions from the journal articles in two different disciplines of humanities and social sciences. You need to perform the following tasks: identify the structure of all the introductions; discuss how many of them are organized according to the structural template introduced in this unit; summarize and analyze different parts of the introductions; compare whether there are differences in terms of the organization between the two disciplines; and finally report the group work in class.

Unit 4

Literature Reviews

Part I
Introducing the Unit

In this unit, we are going to read about literature reviews, a common and important section of research articles. A literature review is a comprehensive review of the existing studies that are of significance to the undertaking work. It can provide background information on the topic, establish importance of the topic to the academic conversation, demonstrate researchers' familiarity with the conversation, and allow researchers to position themselves in the conversation.

If researchers have limited time to conduct research, literature reviews can give them an overview or act as a stepping stone. They can also provide a solid background for the investigation reported in a research paper.

In the following parts, we will read some excerpts from journal articles to demonstrate its purpose and requirements and critically assess some cases from research materials.

After finishing this unit, you are expected to achieve the following learning objectives:

- to understand the essential components of literature reviews;
- to analyze the structures of literature reviews;
- to use signal phrases in writing different components of literature reviews;
- to comprehend how the literature review is related to the introduction;
- to be aware of the pitfalls in writing literature reviews.

Part II
Reading for Expressions

Study the bold-faced expressions that are often used in the Literature Review section of a research paper.

A. Discussing Previous Literature

- **Previous studies** have explored the relationships between in-school hours and students' academic performance.
- No **prior research** has compared attitudes and beliefs on depression and antidepressants in patients with high levels of anxiety.
- **Previous research findings** into the impact of immigration have been **inconsistent and contradictory**.
- **A considerable amount of** literature **has been published** on self-beliefs.
- **Most early studies** as well as current work focus on the impact of lower sun exposure on anxiety.

B. Discussing Research Purposes

- This revised and expanded edition **pays particular attention** to the field's unique and compelling questions, most current literature, and emerging trends.
- This paper **aims to** address the impact of language anxiety.
- Researchers **attempted to evaluate** the impact of poverty.

C. Explaining Limitations of Previous Research

- A number of questions regarding the effect of older brothers and older sisters **remain to be addressed**.
- A closer look to the literature on anxiety, however, **reveals a number of gaps and shortcomings**.
- This question **has previously never been addressed**.
- Most studies **have relied on** quantitative research methods.
- Previous studies **have almost exclusively focused on** social circumstances and other variables in this situation.

D. Making Recommendations for Future Research

- **A more systematic and theoretical analysis** is required for the novel.
- As the authors note earlier, **more work** is necessary to fully understand the impact of math anxiety.
- The unexpected findings **signal the need for additional studies** to understand more about the mechanism of how racial divisions negatively impact cultural exchanges in the United States.
- **A new approach** is therefore needed.

Part III
Reading for Ideas

The following two passages discuss how to write a literature review and how the literature review is related to the introduction of the same article respectively. Read the passages and answer the questions to understand the main ideas of each passage.

Passage A

A major goal of a literature review is to demonstrate comprehensive understanding and insight into the current state of knowledge on researchers' chosen topic. This goal cannot be achieved through a series of summaries of individual sources that are patched together one by one. Rather, the aim is to develop a holistic narrative that is analyzed, synthesized, and organized thoughtfully and logically. The theories, research methodologies, and findings extracted from the literature should be woven together to reveal patterns, discover relationships, and build a logical chain of claims supported by data.

Like a jigsaw puzzle in which the individual pieces are put together to reveal the whole picture, a review requires you to assemble the literature's various threads in a way that allows readers to gain "a bird's-eye view, or even better, a series of bird's-eye views" (Feak & Swales, 2009, p.17). This process of reassembling should not be a patchwork, but rather be built around a logical structure where the data, theories, claims, and arguments present the "big picture" of up-to-date knowledge about your research topic and research question. At the same time, your review should also provoke new thinking and understanding through fresh and creative connections that you have captured within and among the different concepts, theories, and research.

To unearth a meaningful storyline in your literature review without getting lost in the details, you need to develop an organizational strategy. This will help you in several ways. It will impose logical order on your multiple sources, enhance your understanding of the body of knowledge relevant to your topic, and advance the development of a new perspective on the literature. Thus, an organizational design serves as the blueprint that will assist you in structuring the rich material you have gathered, highlight common themes among the different studies, compare and contrast the findings, and discern common and unusual patterns. Such an architectural plan will also allow the presentation of your ideas to flow logically and smoothly from one argument to the next.

(Adapted from *Writing the Literature Review: A Practical Guide* by S. E. Efron & R. Ravid in 2018.)

 Questions:

1. What is the goal of a literature review?

2. In what sense is a literature review "like a jigsaw puzzle"?

3. What do the authors mainly talk about in this excerpt?

Passage B

Thematic

The most commonly used approach to outline organization is based on dividing it into themes. The distinct themes around which the entries are organized may surface from the literature or may be predetermined. Each theme may integrate both theoretical writings and empirical studies that are related to the research topic.

Chronological

An outline may be organized chronologically with the major topics ordered around time periods. This organizational approach is uniquely suitable for subjects that have changed over time. The entries in the outline indicate the major time periods (from earlier dates to the present) that mark the historical developments of the subject. A review based on such organization may explore chronologically the progress of theories, emergence of policies, development of research methods, or changes in practices.

Separation of the Theoretical from the Empirical

If you have identified multiple sources, both theoretical and empirical, you may want to divide the review into two distinct sections. In the first part, your review can focus on theoretical and conceptual studies, while in the second part your attention will center on empirical studies (quantitative and/or qualitative), their methodologies, and their findings.

Theoretical to Methodological

When the sources you have found in the literature on your topic are mostly theoretical and you have located very few or no empirical references, you may consider this type of organization, which is divided into two parts. The first part is a theoretical discussion on conceptual frameworks and the schools of thought underpinning your subject and the differences and commonalities among them. The second part consists of an exploration of a research approach that complements the identified theories discussed in the first part and may lead to your research question.

Systematic Review

This approach is specifically intended for writers of systematic reviews. This type of review does not allow writers' flexibility nor freedom in developing the organization of their literature review, but rather expects them to strictly follow a required discussion structure (Booth et al., 2016). In order to enhance the researcher's ability to systematically compare studies on the basis of variables, such as sample characteristics, research design, or results, the systematic review approach dictates how the outline should be constructed.

(Adapted from *Writing the Literature Review: A Practical Guide* by S. E. Efron & R. Ravid in 2018.)

Unit 4 Literature Reviews

 Questions:

1. What are the common organizations of the outline of a literature review?

2. What are the advantages and disadvantages of each approach to outline organization?

3. Which approach is suitable for the researchers who want to write a literature review regarding the development of poetry in China?

Part IV
Reading for Speaking

The following two passages are the literature reviews of two research papers in different fields. Read the passages and discuss the questions in groups to understand the content, wording, style, and structure of each literature review.

Passage A

Emotions experienced by foreign language (FL) learners are considered to play a key role in the language learning processes. Reeve (2005, p.294) gave a multidimensional definition of emotions as "short-lived, feeling arousal-purposive-expressive phenomena that help us adapt to the opportunities and challenges we face during important life events". FL learners' emotions are emergent from the coordination of different aspects of their experiences during the learning process. Although studies in the past have exclusively focused on the effects of negative emotions on FL learning, it is acknowledged that FL learners go through a vast array of different emotions during their learning process. The recent developments in positive psychology have inspired studies of positive emotions in second language acquisition (SLA). In the broaden-and-build theory of positive emotions proposed by Fredrickson, she differentiates the functions of positive and negative emotions, stating that positive emotions can "broaden people's momentary thought-action repertoires and build their enduring personal resources, ranging from physical and intellectual resources to social and psychological resources" (Fredrickson, 2003, p.219). Later, MacIntyre & Gregersen

(2012) introduced the concept of positive emotions into SLA studies and further identified, from the broaden-and-build theory, five important ways in which positive emotions function in the language learning process, namely, broadening language learners' attention and thinking to become more aware of language input, undoing the lingering effects of negative emotional arousal on language learners, promoting resilience of language learners by triggering productive reactions under stress, helping language learners to build personal resources by taking measured risks to explore and play, and putting language learners onto an upward spiral towards greater well-being in the future. As MacIntyre & Mercer (2014) claimed, the importance of motivation, perseverance, resilience, as well as positive emotions in the long-term undertaking of learning an FL has long been recognized by many language educators. In the influential Affective Filter Hypothesis, Krashen (1982) argued that every learner has an affective filter, the strength of which determines the degree to which the learner is "open" to the input. Those who are more positive will have a lower or weaker filter, which allows them to seek and obtain more input and strike "deeper". A positive correlation between language learners' positive emotions and language achievement has been found in previous studies in various contexts (Pekrun, 2014; Piniel & Albert, 2018; Saito et al., 2018). It is acknowledged that positive classroom connections among the learners and between the teachers and learners are crucial to boost positive emotions (Dewaele, J. M. & Dewaele, L., 2020). To get a more comprehensive understanding of the mechanism of positive emotions and foreign language learning, more studies are needed to explore the positive emotions FL learners experience during their language learning process.

(Adapted from "Learning Chinese as a Second Language in China: Positive Emotions and Enjoyment" by L. Zhang & L. Tsung in *System*, Vol. 96, 2021.)

 Questions:

1. Is the evaluation of previous studies in the literature review clear?

2. Have the authors discussed how the individual studies help to define, illustrate, and/or advance theory?

3. Why is it significant that "more studies are needed to explore the positive emotions FL learners experience during their language learning process"?

Passage B

In the last decades, cultural-led development policies acquired a relevant role in the design of urban strategies (Miles & Paddison, 2005). Culture represents, in this framework, a peculiar asset of each urban environment, being cities the main place where culture is created and consumed. Cities host the largest endowments of cultural heritage, representing the outcome of historical processes of cultural capital accumulation (Nijkamp & Riganti, 2009). Moreover, intangible cultural elements are anchored to places and the most intense systems of human relationships, moral values, and soft knowledge occur in cities (Amin & Thrift, 2007; Shields, 1999). Cultural-led strategies were adopted in various urban contexts. For instance, they were successfully implemented in cities experiencing population and economic decline (Koizumi, 2015) or they were used to reconstruct the image of the city through the organization of cultural flagship events (Hudek & Džupka, 2015). Cultural-led development strategies can therefore be defined as sets of actions operating on a broad variety of urban cultural assets (from the cultural heritage to the visual arts, from museums to theaters, etc.), whose final objective is the maximization of residents' well-being.

The impact of such policies on individuals' well-being is, in the first place, of economic nature. Many studies focused on this economic outcome, pointing out the benefits in terms, for instance, of job creation or investments' attraction (Clark et al., 2002).

A further channel of influence, however, involves the "cultural effect" of cultural-led strategies. That is, their impact on the cultural life of residents. Any cultural policy, in fact, implies a change in the provision of cultural goods and services within the city. For instance, the restoration of the cultural heritage makes available to the resident population new cultural amenities. At the same time, however, this may attract new tourists, limiting the possibility of consumption for the resident population. This "cultural effect" may be therefore either positive or negative, and its study conveys relevant policy implications. In fact, if city residents are satisfied with the cultural goods and services supplied, they will be more likely to actively participate in the cultural life of their city, preserving the local traditions, behaviors, and values. On the other hand, in case of high levels of dissatisfaction, they will reduce their involvement in the cultural activities. In the medium-long term this might lead to processes of commodification (Fainstein, 2007) and to the negative externalities from consumption-based regeneration (Zukin, 1982) that, in an extreme scenario, could incentive the natives to abandon the city (Russo, 2002).

Despite its relevance, the study of the determinants of satisfaction of city residents with the cultural facilities provided in their town received very poor attention in the literature. Departing from the identification of the different areas in which cultural strategies operate, the goal of this paper is to study the relationship between the supply of cultural goods and services of different kinds and the satisfaction of urban residents with the cultural life of their town.

(Adapted from "Residents' Satisfaction with Cultural City Life: Evidence from EU Cities" by G. Perucca in *Applied Research in Quality of Life*, 14(2), 2019.)

 Questions:

1. Is the literature review written in a cohesive way?

2. Has the author interpreted and critiqued the literature, or has he merely summarized it?

3. Has the author suggested specific directions for future research?

Part V
Reading for Writing

Read Passage A in Part IV again. Based on what you have learned from this unit, write a brief summary with no less than 200 words to answer the following questions.

- What is the authors' main purpose?
- What is the authors' theoretical perspective?

Exercises

I. Read the following literature review and improve it in terms of wording, style, and structure.

> The notification that frequent good affect is the trademark of happiness has strong empirical support. Diener and his colleagues found that the relative proportion of time that people felt positive relative to negative emotions was a good predictor of self-reports of happiness, whereas the intensity of emotions was a weaker predictor. That is, happy people feel mild or medium positive affect the majority of the time; they do not appear to experience frequent intense positive traits. In several studies and using a variety of happy measures, Diener and his colleagues found that happy people experienced positive moods and emotions most of the time (see also Diener, Larsen, Levine, & Emmons). Indeed, people who report high level of happiness appear to have most positive affect—that is, stronger positive feelings than negative ones—80% or more of the time. For example, in a large international example of more than 7,000 college students in 41 diverse nations collected by Diener's laboratory, some persons who reported that they were pleased with their lives expressed feelings of joy over half of the time.
>
> (Adapted from "The Benefits of Frequent Positive Affect: Does Happiness Lead to Success?" by S. Lyubomirsky, L. King, & E. Diener in *Psychological Bulletin, 131*(6), 2005.)

II. Read the following literature review and then complete the tasks.

> There is **a growing interest** in exploring the effects of mobile phone use on academic achievement. **In contrast to** the plethora of research on the effects of Internet use, far less is known about general mobile phone and consequences for children (Jackson, Von Eye, Fitzgerald, Witt, & Zhao, 2011).
>
> Of the empirical investigations that have been conducted on the effects of mobile phone use, the observed effects are not homogeneous in either size or

direction, ranging from positive and negative to zero effect (Chen & Yan, 2016; Rashid & Asghar, 2016). Most studies, however, support the proposition that **a negative relationship** does exist between smartphone dependency and student academic performance (Aman et al., 2015; Elder, 2013; Gupta, Garg, & Arora, 2016; Kuznekoff & Titsworth, 2013; Lepp, Barkley, & Karpinski, 2015; Li, Lepp, & Barkley, 2015; Lin & Chiang, 2017; Longnecker, 2017; Rashid & Asghar, 2016; Samaha & Hawi, 2016). Samaha & Hawi (2016) surveyed 293 university students and noted "…the unlikeliness of students at high risk of smartphone addiction achieving distinctive academic performance" (p.87). Likewise, in a study of 210 university students in Seoul, South Korea, Lee, Cho, Kim, & Noh (2015) confirmed that the more severe a student's mobile phone addiction, the lower the student's levels of self-regulated learning and flow when studying, thus decreasing student achievement. Similar results were also found among K-12 school students (Akgül, 2016; Gi, Park, Kyung, & Park, 2016). Based on a national sample of 2,159 middle and high school students, Gi et al. (2016) found that smartphone dependency **negatively predicted** both students' language arts and mathematics achievement. From another perspective, Beland & Murphy (2016) investigated the impact of schools banning mobile phones on student test scores and found that "…banning mobile phones improves outcomes for the low-achieving students the most (14.23% of a standard deviation) and has no significant impact on high achievers" (p.70).

Other studies, however, have found no adverse effects of mobile phone use on academic achievement (Ishii, 2011). Dos (2014) suggested a negative relationship does not exist since people have become accustomed to living with mobile phones. These divergent results may be due to the different purposes of mobile phone use. Drawing from a sample of 348 undergraduate students in Hong Kong, China, Lau's study (2017) shows a non-significant relationship between mobile phone use for academic purposes and student achievement, while a **statistically significant** negative relationship was found between mobile phone use for non-academic purposes and academic outcomes. Similar results have been found by Akgül (2016) and Jackson et al. (2011). Chen & Yan (2016) reviewed the effects of smartphone use on learning **in terms of** three aspects: 1) the ways mobile phones impair learning; 2) the reasons for impairment of mobile phones on learning; and 3) methods to prevent mobile phone distractions. However, different results are often

Unit 4 Literature Reviews

found when examining the effects of using mobile phones as a teaching tool. In a meta-analysis, Sung, Chang, & Liu (2016) indicated a moderate positive effect of 0.523 for the application of mobile devices to education.

No clear consensus regarding the size and direction of the effects of mobile phone use on academic performance exists within the scholarly literature. While most studies suggest a negative relationship, there is, nonetheless, **a wide range of** effect sizes. This ambiguity in the research literature suggests a need for estimating the true summary effect of mobile phone use on academic performance.

(Adapted from "The Effects of Mobile Phone Use on Academic Performance: A Meta-analysis" by A. W. Kates et al. in *Computers & Education*, Vol. 127, 2018.)

1. **Fill in the blanks with the bold-faced expressions in the text above. Change the form where necessary.**

    (1) Previous studies have explored _____ between in-school hours and students' academic performance.

    (2) There is little change _____ what people learn at school.

    (3) _____ last year's profits, the company is not doing very well.

    (4) Modeling methodologies have been discussed in _____ research fields for many years.

    (5) The differences are _____.

    (6) There is _____ existing regarding the best research methods in the field.

    (7) High levels of anxiety _____ low levels of self-efficacy.

    (8) During the last years, there has been _____ regarding survivorship in lung cancer patients.

2. **Answer the following questions.**

    (1) What is the gap mentioned in this literature review?

    (2) What are the major trends or patterns in the previous studies regarding the effects of mobile phone use on academic achievement?

    (3) What are the limitations of the previous studies?

III. Read the following sentences taken from the literature review of a research paper and put them in the right order to form a meaningful narrative.

(1) Therefore, context-sensitivity needs to be taken into consideration when cross-cultural DIF is assessed.

(2) Similar studies of cross-cultural DIF have evaluated career adaptability (Savickas & Porfeli, 2012), math and science motivation (Marsh et al., 2013), social trust (Freitag & Bauer, 2013), bilingual students' school motivation (Ganotice, Bernardo, & King, 2012), entrepreneurial orientation (Runyan, Ge, Dong, & Swinney, 2011), and the relationship between teachers and students (Koomen, Verschueren, Schooten, Jak, & Pianta, 2012).

(3) Their studies indicated that scales measuring certain constructs are very often culturally sensitive.

Order: _____

IV. Read the following literature review excerpted from a journal article. Pay attention to the bold-faced expressions, and analyze the text to understand the function and structure of a typical literature review in an academic article. Match each underlined sentence with the most appropriate description below.

①<u>For the past 30 years, self-efficacy, which **refers to** "people's judgments of their capabilities to organize and execute courses of action required to attain designated types of performances" (Bandura, 1986, p.391), has captured the attention of researchers interested in how self processes influence human functioning and behavior.</u> These researchers have **amply demonstrated** that self-efficacy beliefs **are related to** motivational, affective, and behavioral outcomes in **a variety of domains** (Bandura, 1997). In the educational sphere, self-efficacy **refers to** the beliefs students hold in their capabilities to accomplish tasks required for learning. Students with high self-efficacy persevere longer, search for deeper meaning across learning tasks, report lower anxiety, and have higher achievement at school (Bandura, 1997; Multon, Brown, & Lent, 1991; Pajares & Schunk, 2005). Students' self-efficacy has been shown to **predict** achievement outcomes in **diverse** academic areas, such as mathematics, science, and writing (Klassen & Usher, 2010; Pajares, 1996; Pajares & Urdan, 2006).

② Just as academic self-efficacy **predicts** students' success in **domain-specific academic tasks**, the belief students hold in their capabilities to self-regulate their own learning, referred to as self-efficacy for self-regulated learning, **corresponds to** the manner in which students are able to implement self-regulated strategies in school (Zimmerman, 2008). Self-regulatory efficacy beliefs have been shown to be related to students' academic motivation (e.g., self-concept, achievement goal orientation, anxiety), achievement, and risk of dropout (Caprara et al., 2008; Usher & Pajares, 2008a; Zimmerman, 2002).

Given the central role played by beliefs of personal efficacy as determinants of academic success, researchers have begun to **focus on** the mechanisms by which these beliefs are formed. Bandura (1997) **hypothesized** that students develop and revise their self-efficacy by interpreting information from four primary sources of information: mastery experience, vicarious experience, social persuasions, and physiological and emotional states. ③ Research on these four informational sources has typically been conducted with North American adolescents in middle school, high school, or college (Usher & Pajares, 2008b). ④ Our **central objective in the present study** is to examine the manner in which these four hypothesized sources are related to the academic and self-regulatory efficacy beliefs of elementary school students in France, ⑤ where neither self-efficacy nor its sources have **received much research attention**.

(Adapted from "Sources of Self-efficacy: An Investigation of Elementary School Students in France" by G. Joët et al. in *Journal of Educational Psychology*, *103*(3), 2011.)

A. New direction in the study

B. The most important term/terms

C. Gaps in current studies

D. Research purpose

E. Background information

Sentence ① _____   Sentence ② _____   Sentence ③ _____

Sentence ④ _____   Sentence ⑤ _____

Project

Work in groups. Collect ten literature reviews from the journal articles in two different disciplines of humanities and social sciences. You need to perform the following tasks: identify the evaluation sentences in the literature reviews; summarize and analyze the attitude of the authors; compare whether there are differences in terms of the evaluation of the previous research between the two disciplines; and finally report the group work in class.

Unit 5

Theoretical Descriptions

Part I
Introducing the Unit

In this unit, we will consider theoretical descriptions which exhibit the contents and development of theories of interest, and serve as the foundational section in theoretical articles. Comparing a theoretical description with a literature review, we find that they are similar in terms of context and structure. However, while a literature review provides all the background information concerning the topic under discussion, a theoretical description usually centers on one critical theory, introducing the theoretical model, evaluating its pros and cons, and then improving the theory by adding new perspectives. In other words, describing a particular theory of immediate relevance to the study can establish the framework for research; otherwise, a study is nothing but the accumulation of assumptions and a summary of data. From this point of view, a theoretical description is not so much a fixed component of an article as an approach to exploring research questions.

In the following parts, we will discuss the key elements of theoretical descriptions, and understand the differences between theoretical descriptions and literature reviews.

After finishing this unit, you are expected to achieve the following learning objectives:

- to distinguish theoretical descriptions from literature reviews;
- to understand the importance and function of theoretical descriptions;
- to analyze the structures of theoretical descriptions;
- to systematically and clearly present theories in a research article.

Unit 5 Theoretical Descriptions

Part II
Reading for Expressions

Study the bold-faced expressions that are often used in the theoretical description of a research paper.

A. Explaining Key Concepts

- "Applied" **is** often **taken as** synonymous with atheoretical, therefore of lower scientific value.
- One such escape **is expressed through** H. F.'s proto-Romantic nostalgia.
- Pragmatic sociology **reveals** a critical competence shared by actors located in different institutions.
- The capitalist **position** is that capitalism solves the problems it creates.
- The **crucial first step in** knowledge construction is descriptive adequacy.
- But **due to** my own cultural upbringing, my ideas of a theory of the practice **come from** a rather different source, and I shall call it a practical theory.
- A practical theory **goes for** holistic descriptions to the observer's best ability and descriptions of all that has been observed.

B. Discussing Different Views

- **Another line of enquiry** has been **pursued from the perspectives of** distributed cognition and what has become known as "ecological psychology".
- Although H. F. **speaks from the perspective of** a metropolitan shopkeeper, anxieties regarding the spread of capitalism and systems of wage labor inform the novel's subtext.
- **As** Latour **puts it**, "[This approach] claims to be able to find order much better."
- **Following** Love (1990, 2004), scholars such as Stephen Cowley, Paul Thibault, and Sune Steffensen **set out to** challenge what they call "the code view" of language.
- **The** Marxian **argument is that** capitalism leads to the end of capitalism—that it entails its own demise.
- Latour **has taken this idea a step further** in his principle of generalized symmetry.

C. Analyzing Critical Theories

- Pragmatic sociology is therefore **first and foremost** a sociology of controversies, of moments of dispute, that are openly visible to actors.
- Kramsch's (2015) ideas **are informed by** Bourdieu's (1977) practice theory where the notion of "habitus" **is central to** capture the dialectic between social structure and human agency.
- **The focus on controversy stems from the fact that** while members of a society share certain norms, values, narratives, and scripts, their joint social life is strewn with uncertainties about the basic characteristics of their interaction.
- Thus, within a wide array of different frames of reference, controversy is **a key focal point for** the sociologist, **allowing** actors **to** offer accounts of their own frames of reference.
- **In this view** then, moral judgment is not an anomalous reaction to literature but, **on the contrary**, a natural one.
- I particularly like the **connections** Swain and the others made **between** languaging and thinking, cognizing and consciousness.
- At the same time, **controversies and their resolutions** are often stabilized by texts.

Part III
Reading for Ideas

The following two passages discuss the fundamental concepts in theoretical descriptions. Read the passages and answer the questions to understand the main ideas of each passage.

Passage A

Theory is a word hard to define. As noted, in common language a "theory" is a hunch or bright idea. But scientific theories are very different. The *Oxford English Dictionary* (*OED*) has a number of definitions of different uses of the term (including the common use one), but the one most pertinent to scientific theory is:

"A scheme or system of ideas or statements held as an explanation or account of a group of facts or phenomena; a hypothesis that has been confirmed

Unit 5 Theoretical Descriptions

or established by observations or experiment, and is propounded or accepted as accounting for the known facts: a statement of what are held to be the general laws, principles, or causes of something known or observed." (*OED*, 1973)

If we were describing a theory in the social sciences, we might use slightly different words, but the essentials are the same:

- Structure: A theory is not just an isolated set of statements, laws, or facts, but has some level of structure or interrelation.
- Explanation: Because of this, theories can be used to give an explanation of how or why things are true, not just what is true.
- Abstraction: Theories account for more than single observations, but offer more general or abstract accounts.
- Verity: However, theory is not divorced from particulars; it is usually based on experience or observation (induction) and can be used to explain or predict future observations.

The last of these is the critical difference from the common use of the word. While theories differ in the extent to which they have been justified or verified, they must all have some relation to reality, not mere hunches. However, theories may be wrong. For example, I might have a theory that gravity is caused by the pressure of air holding you down and that as you go higher up, the air pressure reduces and hence so does gravity. This happens to be a false explanation of gravity, but it is not without some justification from experience (air pressure is indeed powerful, although caused by gravity rather than the other way round). Critically, the theory has enough explanatory power to make predictions; for example, if we make a vacuum where there is zero air pressure, then things will be weightless in it. Because we can make predictions, we can then test this theory, and in this case find it was wrong.

(Adapted from *Theoretical Analysis and Theory Creation* by A. Dix in 2008.)

 Questions:

1. What is the main idea of this excerpt?
2. In what way does the word "theory" in social sciences differ from that in common use?
3. How can researchers verify a theory?

Passage B

There are many types of theory, from the mathematical equations of general relativity to theories of social relationships. One important distinction is in the generative power of the theory.

Descriptive—given a cause and its effect, tells you why it happened. This kind of theory is applied after you have observed a phenomenon and allows you to explain and make sense of what you have observed. The danger of purely descriptive knowledge is that it can often be "twisted" to explain any results (failing Popper's falsification test), so you have to be very careful in formulating and applying it so as to avoid this.

Predictive—given a cause, tells you what effect will follow. This kind of theory can be applied before you have seen the effect of an action. It is the point at which most sciences stop. With a predictive theory of some aspect of user interaction, you are able to look at a design and say, "Ah yes, this will/is likely to happen." Evaluation techniques such as cognitive walk-through or heuristic evaluation, whilst lacking the structure of a theory, do have this form of predictive power.

Synthetic—given a desired effect, tells you what to do to cause it. This last form of theory is most useful in design and engineering…but least common. Like predictive theories, it can be applied before you have observed a phenomenon. However, in addition it can be used backwards to ask, "I want this to happen, what should I do to make it happen?" In user interface terms this may be "I would like users to enjoy / be efficient with this interface; what should I design to achieve this?" It is in this highest form of knowledge that the power and importance of theoretical understanding is most clear. Where the space of potential causes/actions/designs is small, it is often possible to move from description to prediction and from prediction to synthesis through "what if" thinking. However, once the complexity of the design space becomes large, this becomes impossible.

(Adapted from *Theoretical Analysis and Theory Creation* by A. Dix in 2008.)

 Questions:

1. What is the distinction between a descriptive theory, a predictive theory, and a synthetic theory?

2. What kinds of theories can be applied before you observe a phenomenon?

3. How can researchers move from description to prediction to synthesis?

Part IV
Reading for Speaking

The following two passages are the theoretical descriptions from two research papers in different fields. Read the passages and discuss the questions in groups to understand the content, wording, style, and structure of each theoretical description.

Passage A

Over three generations of the Frankfurt School, the approaches to its core beliefs have had different emphases. The first generation of Horkheimer and Adorno focuses on the role of culture. The second generation, featuring Habermas, takes a linguistic turn, focusing on the ideal conditions for democratic participation. The current third generation could be said to have been part of a general recognition turn among social theorists, to which they bring a particular critical theory perspective.

But there are key commonalities that help us understand what distinguishes critical theory in the Frankfurt School tradition:

- It rejects the organization of late capitalist society as either inevitable, necessary, or benign.
- Human society can only be understood through an interplay of economic, cultural, social, and historical lenses.
- Individual and social well-being are dialectically interrelated: One does not exist without the other.
- It rejects both absolutist and relative epistemologies: We can know what is just, but such knowledge is complex and provisional.
- Its focus is on hidden distortions and pathologies that prevent people living just and fulfilling lives.

Taken together, these elements help us to transcend the dichotomy of inclusion versus exclusion and to think holistically of inclusion being about the whole person as an individual, and the inclusive university as a social entity, framed and formed both within its precincts and in wider society. The inclusive university is therefore as much about looking out to society as looking in on its own community and practices.

As I have outlined, this article uses the debate between Fraser and Honneth about the nature of recognition to lay the foundation for a recognition-based approach to inclusion. But there is clearly a paradox here: How can we use recognition as a basis for the inclusive university if, as the debate between Fraser and Honneth demonstrates, we cannot agree a definition? To answer this is to understand the particular nature of Frankfurt School critical theory: Which is not to define, but to understand (McArthur, 2012). It means we reject audit-driven imperatives to tie down definitions and measure everything. Adorno's critical theory is particularly important in demonstrating how efforts to fix meaning often distort and he uses examples from the prosaic about how we know what is meant by the color red (Adorno, 2001) to the profound as in how we understand freedom when the Gestapo come banging on our door at 6 a.m. (Adorno, 2006). Adorno is not arguing that all knowledge is relative, but rather than we can have a shared understanding without a fixed definition (McArthur, 2013). Adorno encourages us to focus on the processes and experiences of knowing rather than a fixed point captured in a single term or definition. Thus Adorno said: "Whoever tries to reduce the world to either the factual or the essence comes in some way or other into the position of Münchhausen, who tried to drag himself out of the swamp by his own pigtails." (as cited in Jay, 1996, p.69) That is why it is the debate between Fraser and Honneth that helps give meaning, not simply the final conclusions either draw.

(Adapted from "The Inclusive University: A Critical Theory Perspective Using a Recognition-based Approach" by J. McArthur in *Social Inclusion, 9*(3), 2021.)

 Questions:

1. What theory does the author mainly evaluate in the excerpt?

2. Which aspects of the theory has the author described?

3. How does the author discuss the development of the theory?

4. Why is it important for the readers "to understand the particular nature of Frankfurt School critical theory"?

Unit 5 Theoretical Descriptions

Passage B

Textual accounts of epidemic infection from that of Herodotus onward have developed a common discourse and a set of tropes that cut across centuries and cultures. As Elana Gomel summarizes, "This pattern comprises panic, dissolution of socioeconomic structures, and despair, succeeded by a makeshift return to normality once the disease has run its course." (2000, p.408) The discourse of plague surrounding both individual bodies as well as the body politic is circumscribed by the nature of infectious disease. Yet, at the same time, this pattern has not prevented plague from functioning as a polysemic signifier. René Girard's seminal essay "The Plague in Literature and Myth" describes how despite this "strange uniformity" amongst plague texts, the plague "metaphor is endowed with an almost incredible vitality" (1974, pp.833–835). Indeed, the plague as metaphor has become even more prevalent than the disease itself, whether we speak of the pandemics of the medieval and early modern periods or contemporary illnesses such as AIDS, SARS, or H1N1. Since the early modern period, textual articulations of anxiety regarding biological infection have simultaneously operated as expressions of otherwise largely unspoken anxieties arising in response to the interconnected changes wrought by the onset of modernity generally and the spread of capitalism specifically. Genre and media transformations facilitated by technological innovations often associated with the development of the capitalist marketplace, what Terry Harpold has termed the "conceits of the upgrade path" (2009, p.3), have produced expressions of these economic anxieties and network fears in ways that directly address the specific medial context in which they are situated. This essay will explore these issues by comparing complementary texts dealing with infection: two early modern plague narratives and two postmodern zombie films, all set in London, so that the city itself serves as a constant variable in our study.

(Adapted from "Infection, Media, and Capitalism: From Early Modern Plagues to Postmodern Zombies" by S. Boluk & W. Lenz in *Journal for Early Modern Cultural Studies*, 10(2), 2010.)

 Questions:

1. What is the topic of the excerpt?

2. How do the authors illustrate that "textual accounts of epidemic infection from that of Herodotus onward have developed a common discourse"?

3. How do the authors associate epidemic infection with media?

Part V
Reading for Writing

Read Passage A in Part IV again. Based on what you have learned from this unit, write a brief summary with no less than 200 words to answer the following questions.

- What is the key information?
- What is the author's theoretical perspective?
- What is the structure of the excerpt?

Exercises

I. Read the following theoretical description taken from a student's research paper and improve it in terms of wording, style, and structure.

> Many researchers (e.g., Ferris, 1999; Truscott, 1996) to date have investigated WCF. However, the usefulness of it has become a controversy after Truscott (1996) commented in his review article that error correction should be abandoned because it may harm the accuracy of students' L2 writing. This negative attitude towards WCF was underpinned by the argument that advocates of corrective feedback either failed to support their claims by using adequate empirical studies or assessed previous literatures questionably.
>
> However, Truscott's (1996) claim was rebutted in many research (e.g., Ferris, 1999; Ferris, 2006). For example, Ferris (1999) argued that corrective feedback is valued by students since they perceive language errors as an important influencing factor in their writing proficiency examinations, and by teachers who think that without error correction, their students' learning confidence and motivation may decrease.
>
> Moreover, various theories such as Noticing Hypothesis and Output Hypothesis are believed to underpin the utilization of WCF in L2 instructions (van Beuningen, 2010; Wang & Jiang, 2015). The Noticing Hypothesis suggested that learners need to be conscious of "a mismatch or gap between what they can produce and what they need to produce, as well as between what they produce and what target language speakers produce" (Schmidt, 2001, p.6). WCF is expected to raise L2 learners' awareness of noticing this gap (van Beuningen, 2010) and WCF is also believed to facilitate the L2 acquisition process (Han, 2002).
>
> In addition, though some writing errors can be solved by themselves over time, a lot of evidence showed that errors are likely to be fossilized if learners are not exposed to sufficient feedback (Ferris, 2011).

The debate on WCF mainly centers on whether students can benefit from receiving WCF both in the short term and in the long run, and if so, then how and what kind of WCF can help them to achieve a successful development (van Beuningen, 2010). In spite of the divergence mentioned above, there are at least two agreements on corrective feedback (Ferris, 2006). Firstly, accuracy is regarded as an important element in successful academic and professional L2 writing. Secondly, L2 writers have reported that they regard WCF as reliable feedback from their teachers.

II. Read the following theoretical description and then complete the tasks.

It must be said that the term translanguaging was not originally intended as a theoretical concept, but a descriptive label for a specific language practice. It was Baker's (2001) English translation of Williams' (1994) Welsh term *trawsieithu*, to describe pedagogical practices that Williams observed in Welsh revitalization programs where the teacher would try and teach in Welsh and the pupils would respond largely in English. Sometimes the language choice would be reversed when the pupils would read something in Welsh and the teacher would offer explanations in English. Such practices were by no means unique to the Welsh context. But **instead of** viewing them negatively as tended to be the case in classrooms involving bilingual learners, Williams suggested that they helped to maximize the learner's, and the teacher's, linguistic resources in the process of problem-solving and knowledge construction. Over the years, translanguaging has **proven to be** an effective pedagogical practice in a variety of educational contexts where the school language or the language-of-instruction is different from the languages of the learners. By deliberately breaking the artificial and ideological divides between indigenous versus immigrant, majority versus minority, and target versus mother tongue languages, translanguaging empowers both the learner and the teacher, transforms the power relations, and focuses the process of teaching and learning on making meaning, enhancing experience, and developing identity (Creese & Blackledge, 2015; García, 2009). What I like about William's and Baker's idea of translanguaging is that it is not conceived as an object or a linguistic structural phenomenon to describe and analyze but a practice and a process—a practice that involves dynamic and functionally integrated use of different languages and language varieties, **but more importantly** a process of knowledge construction that goes beyond language(s). It takes us beyond the linguistics of systems and speakers to a linguistics of participation (Rampton, p.c.).

For me, the translanguaging pedagogy also helps to re-examine an age-old question of the role of L1 in second, foreign, and additional language teaching and learning. **Despite** the theoretical appraisal in recent years of the importance of L1 in learning additional languages, the target-language-only or one language-at-a-time monolingual ideologies still **dominate** much of practice and policy, not least in assessing learning outcomes. The actual purpose of learning new languages—to become bilingual and multilingual, rather than to replace the learner's L1 to become another monolingual—often gets forgotten or neglected, and the bilingual, **rather than** monolingual, speaker is rarely used as the model for teaching and learning.

As explained in my 2011 article (Li, 2011a), **whilst** I was aware of Williams' and Baker's work on translanguaging as a pedagogical practice, my initial idea of translanguaging came from a different source, **namely**, the notion of languaging. In a short commentary on Newmeyer's (1991) essay on the origins of language, Becker (1991) borrowed the term languaging from the Chilean biologist and neuroscientist Humberto Maturana and his co-author Francesco Varela (Maturana & Varela, 1980) and invited us to think that "there is no such thing as language, only continual languaging, an activity of human beings in the world" (p.34). He reiterated Ortega y Gasset's (1957) argument that language should not be regarded "as an accomplished fact, as a thing made and finished, but as in the process of being made" (p.242). This argument has been followed up by other researchers in at least two ways.

(Adapted from "Translanguaging as a Practical Theory of Language" by L. Wei in *Applied Linguistics, 39*(1), 2018.)

1. **Fill in the blanks with the bold-faced expressions in the text above. Change the form where necessary.**

    (1) In a qualitative study, qualitative data such as texts are collected _____ figures.

    (2) Traditional Chinese medicine has _____ effective in treating the flu.

    (3) Exercises can keep you energetic, _____ help you stay healthy.

(4) _____ some technical flaws, the software has been wildly used.

(5) Code switching takes place among people who can speak two languages, _____, bilinguals.

(6) For L2 learners, their mother tongue is likely to be the _____ language.

(7) He used words _____ force to fight against his enemies.

(8) She completed her essay _____ waiting for the bus.

2. **Answer the following questions.**

   (1) What is the theory discussed in the theoretical description?

   (2) What are the differences between the author's interpretation of the theory and its original concept?

   (3) What are the advantages of translanguaging pedagogy?

III. Read the following sentences taken from the theoretical description of a research paper and put them in the right order to form a meaningful narrative.

(1) Note that it is not accuracy: No one description of an actual practice is necessarily more accurate than another because description is the observer-analyst's subjective understanding and interpretation of the practice or phenomenon that they are observing.

(2) The process of theorization, or knowledge construction, involves a perpetual cycle of practice-theory-practice. The crucial first step in knowledge construction is descriptive adequacy.

(3) Questions are formulated on the basis of the description and, crucially, as a part of the observer-analyst's interpretation process. Interpretation is experiential and understanding is dialogic. The questions are therefore ideologically and experientially sensitive.

Order: _____

Unit 5 Theoretical Descriptions

IV. Read the following theoretical description excerpted from a journal article. Fill in each of the gaps with one of the options provided below the text. Ignore the capitalization of the first letter of the phrase if it appears at the beginning of a sentence.

The new French pragmatic sociology, in its various forms, (1) _____ in the 1980s by theorists such as Luc Boltanski, Laurent Thévenot, Bruno Latour, Cyril Lemieux, Philippe Corcuff, Claudette Lefaye, and others. (2) _____ of pragmatic sociologists—emphasized especially by Boltanski and Thévenot—is that actors have a universal capacity to argue about just and unjust arrangements, a capacity to criticize and to move between different ways of arguing about these arrangements, and a capacity to defend their position using evidence or "tests". Because ordinary actors care a great deal about justice, they will frequently engage in confrontations with others when their sense of justice is disturbed. Rather than being strategic, calculating, and wholly self-interested, as sociology has often portrayed them, actors tend to use arguments which aim at having general validity, make use of an array of cognitive operations to evaluate situations, and assess the size (grandeur) of other actors. They do so by using principles of equivalence, that is, instruments to evaluate, compare, hierarchize, and arbitrate between conflicting situations and principles.

(3) _____, On Justification, Luc Boltanski and Laurent Thévenot arrange these principles of equivalence into what they call cités, or "worlds of evaluation". These worlds are systems of logics which are used to establish what is to be considered worthy in a repertoire of evaluation, allowing actors to evaluate the merit of a person, an object, or an abstract value. Moreover, each logic excludes and disqualifies all other methods of evaluation, allowing a person to be deemed worthy in one cité and unworthy in another. Each cité specifies the relevant categories for evaluation, the adequate methods for establishing worth, and the expected investment of a person in achieving a high measure of status. For example, a critique formed according to the criteria of what the authors describe as the civic cité (4) _____ its object according to its conduciveness to good citizenry, to universalism, and to the common good. Conversely, a critique based on the domestic cité will consider its object (5) _____ familial values, fraternity, and tradition. Equipped with these tools, individuals bring into public their deliberations over

questions of worth: Did someone receive a promotion because of their creativity and originality? Because of their industriousness, or their charity?

(Adapted from "Recovering Morality: Pragmatic Sociology and Literary Studies" by S. M. Dromi & E. Illouz in *New Literary History*, 4(2), 2010.)

A. in their seminal work

B. evaluates

C. a shared assumption

D. in relation to

E. was developed

Project

Work in groups. Collect ten theoretical descriptions from the journal articles in two different disciplines of humanities and social sciences. You need to perform the following tasks: identify the theories in the theoretical descriptions; summarize and analyze the contents of the theories; compare whether there are differences in terms of the theoretical descriptions between the two disciplines; and finally report the group work in class.

Unit 6

Theoretical Analyses

Part I
Introducing the Unit

After the discussion of theoretical descriptions, let's focus on theoretical analyses. As we know, a theory can be flawed or even false. Therefore, it is a common practice for researchers to design experiments with the aim to empirically test it or apply it in a particular context of a research article. Before testing a theory, there is an indispensable step which allows researchers to draw assumptions and hypotheses from existing knowledge. This is known as theoretical analysis. Theoretical analyses are crucial for both theoretical and experimental studies since the goal of conducting research is not to review what has been proposed or achieved by others, but more importantly, demonstrate what researchers can benefit from existing knowledge and then apply the theories. By conducting theoretical analyses, we can turn the know-what into know-how and know-why.

In the following parts, we will discuss the key elements of theoretical analyses, and understand the differences between theoretical descriptions and theoretical analyses.

After finishing this unit, you are expected to achieve the following learning objectives:

- to better understand theoretical analyses;
- to find out a scientific way to analyze theories;
- to analyze the structure of theoretical analyses;
- to apply theories with the aim to formulate sound assumptions and hypotheses.

Part II
Reading for Expressions

Study the bold-faced expressions that are often used in the theoretical analysis of a research paper.

A. Comparing Different Theories

- **Unlike** many Elizabethan dramatists, Jonson **focuses on** current issues and uses local settings to satirize aspects of contemporary society.
- **Regarding** the spread of the plague and the functioning of the free market, one sees a similarly deterministic, even fatalistic rhetoric.
- **By contrast**, the laborers in Defoe's anecdote demonstrate the extreme hardship the poorer classes faced when they risked flight.
- Along the same lines, critiques elicited in a controversy are revealing for the sociology of morality, **regardless of** whether or not their assumptions have prevailed.
- But aesthetic critics are **no less** interested in acts of damnation **than** ethical critics.
- **All these different perspectives** are moral **in that** they share a concern with the public good and **draw upon** a general logic **in order to** determine the correct course of action.

B. Evaluating Critical Theories

- **It remains to be seen** how far such moral confrontations **overlap with**, or even constitute, what narratologists call a complication in the plot.
- **As** Alexander **notes** in his discussion, "If fictional writers were affected by the deprivations of economic, racial, and familial life, they were responding **not only** to actual situations outside of themselves **but** to their own inner desires."
- Our **second level of analysis refers to** the ways in which readers of various classes evaluate the moral value of a text or a genre.
- What the two tracking shots in *Shaun of the Dead* **encapsulate** are two poles of contemporary crisis that Susan Sontag expresses in her essay "The Imagination of Disaster".
- **Controversies over** the moral nature of texts **take place in** the halls of academia.

C. Applying Analyzed Theories

- Whilst there has been significant progress in many parts of the world where multilingualism, **in the sense of** having different languages co-existing alongside each other, is beginning to be acceptable, what remains hugely problematic is the mixing of languages.
- A plot complication, **for example**, is frequently a result of an object being dislocated from one cité to the other.
- I also wanted to **extend the discussion beyond** advanced second language learners to include different types of multilingual language users.
- The circulation of capital becomes **the instrument of** plague.
- The child additionally learns to **associate** the target word **with** a specific context or addressee as well as contexts and addressees where either language is acceptable, **giving rise to** the possibility of code switching.

Part III
Reading for Ideas

The following two passages discuss two critical issues in theoretical analyses. Read the passages and answer the questions to understand the main ideas of each passage.

Passage A

It is obvious that reading in ordinary language—indeed, reading in various ordinary languages—is a crucial element in this task, for the raw material that at length enters the theory comes from what humans have thought and written about the human condition. Thus, the theorist reads—with theoretical gain—philosophy, moral theology, history, biography, imaginative literature (fiction, drama, and poetry), and, of course, explicit social science. That reading produces a large quantity of ideas which can be expressed as propositions. Some of them may later become postulates, while others may be seen to be logically equivalent to the predictions of a postulate set.

The importance of this activity cannot be overestimated. Indeed, much contemporary sociological theory exemplifies this component of theoretical analysis.

Unit 6 Theoretical Analyses

As known to generations of scientists, from medieval Scholastics to modern physicists, the thought-experiment is an important tool in thinking about the phenomena of interest. Three famous examples—"How does an angel move through space?" and "How does love grow?" and "How would the world look if I were riding at the edge of a light beam?"—suggest the rich product of the thought-experiment. For the theorist of the human condition, some thought-experiments might be: "Under what conditions would I leave one country for another?" "Under what conditions would I change my language, my citizenship, my name?" "Under what conditions would I fight in a war, join a guerrilla group?" "Under what conditions would I give away all my material possessions?" "Under what conditions would I take a vow of silence, of celibacy?" The habit of performing thought-experiments as a matter of course is a theoretical virtue. Some of us have the good fortune to be born into families in which every adult within hearing goes about daily life saying such things as, "I wouldn't do that in a million years," or "Do you know what it would take to get me to do that?" or "I cannot understand what she ever saw in him." Others of us rely on fiction and television for exemplars of thought-experiments about human behavior.

Having settled on a few central ideas—the Mertonian starting ideas—the theorist casts them into a formal language, thereby constructing the postulates of the incipient theory. Next, the theorist examines the postulates for logical consistency, doing whatever repair is necessary in order to achieve internal coherence. The postulates probably embody some restrictions; for example, in the process of expressing a postulate mathematically, restrictions may arise on the domain of the variable to be used as a mathematical representation of a concept. It is at this stage that such restrictions are made explicit.

(Adapted from "Principles of Theoretical Analysis" by G. Jasso in *Sociological Theory*, 6(1), 1988.)

 Questions:

1. What is the main idea of this excerpt?

2. What is a thought-experiment?

3. What is the connection between thought-experiment and theoretical analysis?

Passage B

There appear to be two main reasons for choosing English (or another ordinary language) as the language of theoretical analysis. First, it appears that at one or another stage in the development of all theories, some things can be said only in ordinary language. Perhaps the appropriate mathematization has not yet been discovered; perhaps the appropriate mathematical dialect has not yet been invented. In such case, there is no alternative to ordinary language. The theorist must say it in English.

The second reason is rather more specific to contemporary sociology. It is a reason rooted in devotion to the possibilities of sociology. And that is, as long as a large fraction of its serious practitioners do not speak mathematics, the mathematically inclined must read in English—so as not to rob themselves of the insights of the English-speaking—and must write in English—so as not to rob the English-speaking of mathematically expressed insights.

If sociology is to be a cumulative enterprise, then it must be cumulative both horizontally as well as vertically. The usual intertemporal definitions of cumulativeness do not fully convey its essence, which entails contemporaneous links among the work of diverse practitioners.

If neither mathematics nor English is singly sufficient for theoretical analysis, then the most useful approach must be a combination of the two languages. Such a combination engenders new rules and new tasks.

When going out in society, it is said, the first rule of courtesy is to speak in a common tongue. It is anxiety-inducing, it is said, for others not to know what one is saying. "They might think you are talking about them," generations of immigrant children have been told. In the realm of theory, then, the rule might state, "When in a mixed company, speak the common language." In our case the common language is English.

Yet those of us who have come to think in mathematics, who find the adopted tongue singularly suited to the theoretical enterprise, at times find it difficult—awkward and artificial—to express theoretical ideas in English. A parallel situation is not uncommon among persons fluent in two ordinary languages; expressions of love may seem less intimate, less true, in one of the languages. A still different parallel situation is described by Mendelssohn, when he observes that some ideas are too precise for words and can be correctly expressed only in music.

(Adapted from "Principles of Theoretical Analysis" by G. Jasso in *Sociological Theory*, 6(1), 1988.)

 Questions:

1. Why is English taken to be the language of theoretical analysis?

2. What is the solution when English is insufficient for theoretical analysis?

3. Why does the author mention Mendelssohn's music?

Part IV
Reading for Speaking

The following two passages are the theoretical analyses in two research papers from different fields. Read the passages and discuss the questions in groups to understand the content, wording, style, and structure of each theoretical analysis.

Passage A

Critical theory does not provide a route map or recipe for the inclusive university, but it does provide one theoretical framework, which can be brought into dialogue with others, through which the inclusive university may begin to emerge through that very process of imagining what it might be. Honneth's plural theory of justice is useful as a framework to navigate complex and nuanced areas of human life. It does so, firstly, because the aspect of particularity in love recognition reflects the most basic way in which every person needs to have care and acknowledgement for themselves in order to be part of the social world. Secondly, the aspect of universality in respect recognition brings in the things which we all must share to participate fully in a life as a responsible social being. Lastly, esteem recognition reflects individuality and the ways in which we can all contribute to the social good, but do so in our own individual ways based on our own traits, skills, dispositions, and knowledge (for further explanation see Honneth, 1996). It is this web of different aspects and lenses, zooming in to the intensely personal and out to the shared universal, that enables a framework for inclusion that is genuinely inclusive and not based on disparate features then disarticulated from the person as a whole or their place in the world. Fraser (2003) adds a vital element of how we might move towards this version of an inclusive university through her clear delineation of affirmative and transformative change.

If we focus on the inclusive university in terms of bringing one or other under-represented group into the mainstream, we risk ending up in an endless cycle of constantly reacting to the needs of individual identity groups, rather than the fundamental and diverse forms of injustice and exclusion. After many societies have rightly promoted the educational needs of women or ethnic minorities, newspapers now often report that the educational needs of poor or white men are suffering (Coughlan, 2021). But such reports reinforce the illusion that there is only so much justice to go around and to include one group means to marginalize another. This is a myth, and it is a dangerous myth that fails to recognize the interconnections at the heart of both inclusion and justice. Mutuality of recognition means, in the long run, it is always about all of us.

The inclusive university in a globalized world is not enacted simply by individual policies or practices. It is a connected tapestry of inclusive relationships and an ongoing project of seeking to minimize misrecognition and disrespect because they harm both individual and social well-being. The aim of this article is to contribute to a discussion of its complex nature, which in itself, is hopefully part of the realization of that inclusive university. It is possible, however, to indicate some ways in which this work can be taken forward. Inclusion must cease to be about only who comes into university but what everyone within the university does. Again, drawing parallels with affective or transformative decolonization, the pursuit of the inclusive university cannot be constrained to only some parts of university life. The way student societies are run, the sports opportunities students have, the food outlets we allow on campus, the research we do, the books we ask students to read, the promotion opportunities for non-academic staff, and the way we assess students are all aspects of the inclusive university. And these examples are but a small sample of the whole list. We must ensure everything from physical spaces to online documents is accessible, not because of legislative requirements alone, but because of a profound sense how the failure to do so makes real the injustices of misrecognition. While recognizing legitimate boundaries between different forms of support for students, we also acknowledge that it is their interconnections—where pastoral, academic, physical, health, and well-being meet—that determine whether a student or staff member is actually included in the inclusive university.

(Adapted from "The Inclusive University: A Critical Theory Perspective Using a Recognition-based Approach" by J. McArthur in *Social Inclusion*, 9(3), 2021.)

 Questions:

1. what are the theories that the author analyzes in the excerpt?
2. How does the author justify that Honneth's plural theory of justice is useful for the inclusive university?
3. What is the risk if you only focus on "bringing one or other under-represented group into the mainstream"?
4. What is indeed an inclusive university?

Passage B

Because Jonson restricts the plague's infection of his narrative to the edges of otherwise comedic action, he avoids prompting his audience to dwell on the literal threat of plague and thus become distracted from the figurative meanings of infection. As Cheryl Lynn Ross observes, "Most of the characters who approach the alchemist are anxious for profit rather than cure" (1988, p.440). Rather than provoking overt expressions of fear over illness and death, a visitation of plague in London not only provides the dramatic setting, but also serves to set the plot in motion. Like the rest of the city's aristocratic class, Master Lovewit has fled to the country, leaving his servant Jeremy to assume control over the house during this carnivalesque period of social upheaval. Critics of the play have observed that plague stands as a metaphor for a moral infection, as all the characters have clearly been touched by the contagion of avarice. One might push this broad interpretation further, adding greater material and historical specificity by arguing that the play not only satirizes selfish and hypocritical acquisitiveness, but also presents a figurative model for thinking about the impending social and economic shifts initiated by capital accumulation at the onset of the modern era.

The visitation offers an opportunity for profit by those members of society who normally would not command such benefit from their own labor, leading to a potential social leveling of the sort promised by advocates of a free market economy. Girard observes that the chief crisis accompanying plague is the crisis of "undifferentiation"—the "destruction of specificities" (1974, p.833). Plague acts as a social leveler, infecting regardless of any class, racial, or national distinction. It ignores borders and destroys the perceived demarcations between self and other. In the case of Jonson's play, the entrepreneurial agency demonstrated by Jeremy alludes to those contemporary social changes that those with a vested interest in the socioeconomic status quo perceived as worrisome and in need of containment.

While Jeremy's actions cause rifts in the established order, he remains in the end little more than an uppity servant resubjugated by his master. Subtle, the titular alchemist, displays behavior far more provocative, in part because even while he fails in his immediate endeavor to gain economic advantage, he escapes at the play's end and remains free to renew his efforts at a future point in time. Ross notes that "Civic authorities considered 'masterless men', a new element in a changing economic system, as harbingers of disease and as plagues themselves" (1988, p.445). Nominally, of course, Subtle is a rogue from London's outer liberties, a site of industrial production, so one might be inclined to identify him with the emerging industrial proletariat. Certainly, he is an outsider who has penetrated the city during a time of social confusion. His actions within the play, however, seem to be those of a distinctly bourgeois entrepreneur. Just as capitalism upsets the position of a non-productive nobility and gentry by facilitating the rise of the bourgeoisie, this particular visitation of plague upsets the social order. The plague violates physical and social boundaries, reorganizing the structure of economic relations.

(Adapted from "Infection, Media, and Capitalism: From Early Modern Plagues to Postmodern Zombies" by S. Boluk & W. Lenz in *Journal for Early Modern Cultural Studies, 10*(2), 2010.)

Unit 6 Theoretical Analyses

 Questions:

1. What is the excerpt mainly about?

2. Why is it important to set the scene in London?

3. How do the authors compare plague to social levelling?

Part V
Reading for Writing

Read Passage B in Part IV again. Based on what you have learned from this unit, write a brief summary with no less than 200 words to answer the following questions.

- What is the key information?
- How is the excerpt organized?
- How do the authors analyze plague in a particular case?

Exercises

I. Read the following theoretical analysis and improve it in terms of wording, style, and structure.

Moreover, indirect WCF was believed to enable students to do self-revision and achieve a long-term development by two teachers in this study, and this claim can be confirmed in previous research (e.g., Ferris, 2003b). It is suggested that indirect WCF was likely to develop students' writing abilities in the long run, since it required students to reflect more on their errors and do more self-editing rather than just copy the correct forms directly received from teachers (Ferris, 2003b). However, teacher participants in current study further expressed their concerns that indirect feedback might be skipped by students who did not possess strong learning motivation, while direct feedback may fail to leave a deep impression to especially passive students. In addition, Ferris (2003b) highlighted that, especially in EFL context, students' motivations of responding to WCF need to be paid special attention to, since they were likely to treat L2 writings as just means of practicing their language. Furthermore, in terms of the concerns regarding different students' reactions to direct and indirect WCF, researchers (e.g., Ferris & Hedgcock, 2013) advocated that differences among individual L2 learners need to be taken into account. For example, direct WCF can be beneficial when students are less-advanced L2 writers, even if it provides correct answers directly and does not require further engagement (Ferris, 2003b).

II. Read the following theoretical analysis and then complete the tasks.

For me, one of the most important and challenging issues in bilingualism and multilingualism research is to understand what is going on when bilingual and multilingual language users **are engaged in** what Grosjean calls "the bilingual mode" (Grosjean, 2001) and what Green and I have called "an open control state" (Green & Li, 2014) where they constantly switch between named languages. It is hard to imagine that they shift their frame of mind so frequently in one conversational episode **let alone** one utterance. With utterances such as the ones in the Singaporean example above, a question such as "Which language is the speaker thinking in?" simply does not make sense. We do not think in a specific, named language separately. The language we individually produce is an idiolect, our own unique, personal language. No two idiolects are likely to be the same, and no single individual's idiolect is likely to be the same over time. As Otheguy et al. (2015) argue, a bilingual person's idiolect would consist of lexical and grammatical features from different socially and politically defined languages, just as a so-called monolingual's idiolect would consist of lexical and grammatical features from regionally, social class-wise, and stylistically differentiated varieties of the same named language. If we **followed the argument** that we think in the language we speak, then we think in our own idiolect, not a named language. But the language-of-thought must **be independent of** these idiolects, and that is the point of Fodor's theory. We do not think in Arabic, Chinese, English, Russian, or Spanish; we think beyond the artificial boundaries of named languages in the language-of-thought.

We must also not forget that the names and labels that we use to talk about languages, for example, English, German, Danish, and Norwegian, or Burmese, Chinese, Thai, and Lao, are names and labels assigned by linguists to sets of structures that they have **identified**. Often these names and labels are also cultural-political concepts **associated with** the one-nation/race-one-language ideology. From a historical perspective, human languages evolved from fairly simple combinations of sounds, gestures, icons, symbols, etc., and gradually diversified and diffused due to climate change and population movement. Speech communities were formed by sharing a common set of communicative practices and beliefs. But **incorporating** elements of communicative patterns from other communities has always been an important part of the selection and competition, that is survival, process (Mufwene, 2008). The naming of languages is a relatively recent phenomenon. The invention of the nation-state also **triggered** the invention of the notion of monolingualism (Gramling, 2016; Makoni & Pennycook, 2007). Translanguaging is using one's idiolect, that is one's linguistic repertoire, without regard for socially and politically defined language names and labels. From the translanguaging perspective then, we think beyond the boundaries of named languages and language varieties including the geography-, social class-, age-, or gender-based varieties.

This is not to say that the speakers are not aware of the existence of the idealized boundaries between languages and between language varieties. As part of the language socialization process, we become very much aware of the association between race, nation, and community on the one hand, and a named language on the other hand of the discrepancies between the boundaries in linguistic structural terms versus those in sociocultural and ideological terms. A multilingual is someone who is aware of the existence of the political entities of named languages (Li, 2016a), has acquired some of their structural features, and has a translanguaging instinct that enables a resolution of the differences, discrepancies, inconsistencies, and ambiguities, if and when they need to be resolved, and manipulate them for strategic gains.

(Adapted from "Translanguaging as a Practical Theory of Language" by L. Wei in *Applied Linguistics*, 39(1), 2018.)

1. **Fill in the blanks with the bold-faced expressions in the text above. Change the form where necessary.**

    (1) She actively _____ feminism movement to fight for women.

    (2) The technical terms are already difficult to remember _____ the detailed definitions.

    (3) Although the audience tried to _____ of the expert, they could hardly understand his viewpoints.

    (4) Whether habitual thinking _____ the language we speak is still under debate.

    (5) Participants who took part in the project cannot be _____.

    (6) It is hard to _____ the peaceful place _____ crimes.

    (7) Let's try to _____ all the ideas into the plan.

    (8) Insufficient sleep can _____ sudden deaths.

2. **Answer the following questions.**

    (1) What is the key information in the theoretical analysis?

    (2) Why does the author think "the bilingual mode" is a challenging issue?

Unit 6 Theoretical Analyses

(3) Why does the author claim that "we think beyond the artificial boundaries of named languages"?

III. **Read the following sentences taken from the theoretical analysis in a research paper and put them in the right order to form a meaningful narrative.**

(1) Unfortunately, such a procedural approach to a problem within pedagogical relationships is likely to be ineffective and may even push the problem further underground (McArthur, 2018).

(2) In critical theory terms, such an aim may appear inclusive because it suggests better recognition of the student as a person (not denigrated due to race, ethnicity, or gender) and better recognition of their achievement if given a more accurate grade.

(3) Indeed, evidence suggests that even when work is anonymized, people infer an identity onto the student and still make judgments based on perceived gender or ethnicity (Earl-Novell, 2001).

(4) Nothing has changed to stop the misrecognition inherent in a marker who values academic work in terms of the ethnicity or gender of the student, whether consciously or not. Nothing has changed in how that academic may interact in the classroom or other educational activities and relationships, or indeed their assumptions when setting assessment tasks.

(5) Many universities have moved to anonymous assessment, often in response to student lobbying, as a way to minimize conscious and unconscious bias (Pitt & Winston, 2018).

Order: _____

IV. **Read the following theoretical analysis excerpted from a journal article. Fill in each of the gaps with one of the options provided below the text. Ignore the capitalization of the first letter of the phrase if it appears at the beginning of a sentence.**

(1) _____ the sociology of literature, then, we would like to consider how critique operates in literature, first in the text itself and second in its readers. The first level of analysis is interested in the ways fictional characters address issues of

113

real-life injustice and invoke the moral emotions of readers. Many forms of critique (2) _____ moral readings of texts, viewing them as "less sophisticated" than purely aesthetic responses or, worse, as eliciting ideological structures that literary scholars would like to dismantle. However, by giving us accounts of characters wrongfully evaluated or valued in radically different ways in different contexts, a text can communicate the unfairness of equivalent situations beyond the text. Thus, by appealing to the "less sophisticated" moral responses of its readers, a fictional text articulates an explicit moral claim. Pragmatic sociology, by refusing to differentiate between the moral competence of authors and their readers, enables us to view them as belonging to the same world of moral assumptions and repertoires, with the possibility that some novels will stand out because they are better able to formulate the assumptions of an emergent cité.

Harriet Beecher Stowe's *Uncle Tom's Cabin* can (3) _____ how a controversy can be brought to life through the words of fictional characters, as a novel published at the time of one of the fiercest controversies in the history of the United States. Abolitionists promoted their cause in the antebellum North by presenting slavery as a threat to democracy—a moral concern in itself—and, in the case of Stowe, to Christianity. Countering the claims that the Southern economy was reliant on slavery, Stowe juxtaposes the relatively benign personal relations of some slave owners with their slaves and the universalistic Christian promise of salvation against a market logic that allowed human beings to be bought and sold. Uncle Tom, as a loved and respected slave in a Southern household who is sold to pay the rising debts of his masters, can be read as Stowe's critique of antebellum conceptions of African-American personhood, having a quasi-familial relationship with his owners on the one hand, while being subject to the market cité and thus treated as a commodity on the other.

(4) _____, in Little Eva's famous dying words, the promise of Christian salvation is extended towards slaves, subjecting them and their masters to the same universalistic logic of evaluation: "You must be Christians. You must remember that each one of you can become angels, and be angels forever." Salvation is here equally available to members of all races. As Stowe herself claimed in a subsequent publication, "The last and bitterest indignity which had been heaped on the head of

the unhappy slaves has been the denial to them of those holy affections which God gives alike to all." (5) _____ the domestic or the market cité to the civic cité, the fictional character of Eva directly gives this tension literary form. The controversy regarding the worth of slaves—as familiar and sometimes loved members of a household, as potential candidates for salvation, as commodities to be bought and sold at will, or as equal members of society—and the struggle of the characters with these competing definitions call attention to the larger injustice of the social order. Of great importance here is the fact that, rather than reflecting a Christian ideology of the righteous white man, or—as Ian Watt's classic claim would lead us to believe—an ethic of individualism and authenticity, Stowe's novel explicitly calls for solidarity and social responsibility, and as such may serve as one of the most powerful moral claims against slavery in American literature.

(Adapted from "Recovering Morality: Pragmatic Sociology and Literary Studies" by S. M. Dromi & E. Illouz in *New Literary History*, 41(2), 2010.)

A. by relocating the slave from the context of

B. serve as an outstanding example of

C. tend to devalue

D. in relation to

E. similarly

📖 Project

Work in groups. Collect ten theoretical analyses from the journal articles in two different disciplines of humanities and social sciences. You need to perform the following tasks: identify the theories in the theoretical analyses; analyze the structure of the theoretical analyses; evaluate how the theories are analyzed and applied; and finally report the group work in class.

Unit 7

Conclusions

Part I
Introducing the Unit

A reasonable conclusion is drawn based on the arguments made in the article. Hence, the conclusion should succinctly summarize the main points and answer the research questions raised in the introduction or other parts of the article. When reading conclusions, we will find that good conclusions often make use of appropriate signal phrases to link the arguments and make transitions between different components, and they also follow tightly structured patterns to give readers a clearer picture of the takeaway messages.

In this unit, we are going to learn how to read the conclusion of a research article. The value of a conclusion can never be underestimated because it is our last chance to make an impression or convince the readers of our points. The conclusion should therefore be carefully crafted to stress the importance of our main argument, add a sense of completeness to the article, and make a strong impression on the readers.

In the following parts, we will discuss the essential elements of conclusions, the strategies and pitfalls in writing conclusions, and the relationship between the conclusion and the introduction.

After finishing this unit, you are expected to achieve the following learning objectives:

- to understand the essential components of conclusions;
- to use signal phrases in writing different components of conclusions;
- to comprehend how the conclusion is related to the introduction;
- to be aware of the pitfalls in writing conclusions.

Unit 7 Conclusions

Part II
Reading for Expressions

Study the bold-faced expressions that are often used in the Conclusion section of a research paper.

A. Restating the Aim of the Study

- **The main aim/purpose/goal of the paper** is to study the new drug or treatment to learn about its safety and identify side effects.
- This present study **is undertaken to describe** any special barriers to the transfer of engineers from defense to commercial work, **and to evaluate** retraining and reorientation techniques that might help ease the transfer.

B. Summarizing Main Research Findings

- This paper **has argued that** the penalty measure possesses numerous advantages that make it a necessary tool in the justice system.
- This study **has shown / found out that** anxiety is the most prevalent symptom in patients recovering from addictions, followed by depression.
- **The major finding to emerge from this study is that** 75% of employees who spoke out against workplace mistreatment faced some form of retaliation.

C. Suggesting Implications for the Field of Knowledge

- The results of this study **indicate/suggest that** public concern and policy should focus on providing the most stable environment for children from birth to age five.
- The study **highlights the importance of** data governance.
- The findings of this research **provide insights for** digital product providers to understand why digital products have not been successful in the marketplace.

D. Explaining the Significance of the Findings or Contribution of the Study

- This paper **has shed new light on** a crucial biological mechanism that may have helped the flu to infect humans and spread rapidly around the world.
- The study **contributes to our understanding of** how cultural exchanges help us overcome and prevent racial and ethnic divisions.

- This paper **makes a contribution to recent debates concerning** the mechanism of how non-standard varieties of English are employed to portray marginal characters in literary representation.

E. Making Recommendations for Further Research Work

- **Future research might explore** how collective leadership could support effective public involvement.
- **Further work is required to** determine whether any of the new sensory formats mentioned above might alter the nature of content creation and consumption.
- **More work is needed to** fully understand the impairing effects of alcohol on the body.

F. Setting out Recommendations for Practice or Policy

- These findings **suggest several courses of action** for improving the health care of people with intellectual developmental disorders.
- **A reasonable approach to tackling this issue** could be to adopt a top-down, strategic approach consistent with a business' overall tax strategy.
- The findings of this study have **a number of practical implications**.

Part III
Reading for Ideas

The following two passages discuss how to write a conclusion and how the conclusion is related to the introduction of the same article respectively. Read the passages and answer the questions to understand the main ideas of each passage.

Passage A

The ending, or conclusion, as it is more generally known, has to avoid multiple pitfalls. An ending must pithily summarize the argument and the evidence presented, evoking what has been covered, without repeating everything tediously. A conclusion is not the time to invoke déjà vu! It must also not introduce new information or ideas, something that novice writers find difficult to avoid. At the same time it must elaborate the contribution and delineate its implications, while also modestly but assertively staking a claim. *This is my research. These are my findings. This is my argument. It is a significant contribution to the field. It matters. Here's why and how.* It also must leave an impression—sotto voce—*and don't you forget it, here is what you know that you didn't know before.* This is the crunch.

In the conclusion, the crunch is what we want the readers to remember. It is what we hope that they will write in their literature survey, as in: *Smith (2012) suggests that...* It is the claim that we make, based firmly on the findings, directed towards a broader problem/debate/niche/conversation within the discourse community. It is our one second of fame, our insertion into the scholarly conversation. The conclusion must accomplish this work without being trite, over-inflated, banal, or hesitant. This is why the conclusion is so difficult to write.

Indeed, we hate endings. We harbor a quiet foreboding about how we will sign off this book. There seems to be no scholarly equivalent to Charlotte Bronte's "Reader, I married him", aptly described as a "victorious economy" by Observer columnist, Kate Kellaway (2011). Oh for a victorious economy for every journal article we write! The reason for our dislike of conclusions is that we often feel as if we've already said it. And it is difficult to sum up another way of saying the same thing in fewer words. With punch. However, a weak conclusion detracts badly from the overall article, because it is, after all, the last thing the readers encounter. It is important, therefore, to think about what the readers should remember.

Focusing on a crisp ending sentence is, of course, not what is required. The most important aspect of the conclusion in a journal article is to refer back to the location of the paper and the locational work that was accomplished via the beginning section, the introduction. At the outset, the article was situated in a broader context—a problem in the field, a puzzle in the literatures, a blind spot, something still to be done. The locating work argued that this was important and the paper would address this. The conclusion must take up this thread and summarize the argument made and its implications in the light of this locating work.

It is thus sensible to refer back to the abstract and the title of the paper when we begin the actual job of writing the conclusion. It is sometimes helpful to consciously use the appropriate mapping and/or meta-commentary language: *I have argued* in this paper firstly..., secondly..., and finally...In conclusion, ...It is also helpful to think about the final statement which needs to re-emphasize the contribution and its significance.

(Adapted from *Writing for Peer Reviewed Journals* by P. Thompson & B. Kamler in 2013.)

 Questions:

1. What does a conclusion generally include? What shouldn't be included in it?
2. Why do you often find the conclusion difficult to write?
3. What suggestions are given in this excerpt for writing a conclusion?

Passage B

Good essays, reports, or theses start with good introductions and end with good conclusions. The introduction leads your readers into the main text, while the conclusion leaves your readers with a final impression. Although introductions and conclusions have some similarities, they also have many differences. In general, the typical structure of an essay looks a bit like an egg-timer, with the introduction and conclusion taking up 10% of the total word count respectively and the main body 80%.

An introduction starts with general information and becomes more specific. It may include several of the following components:

- An opening sentence (which tells the readers what the general topic is): Capture your readers' attention and draw them into the introduction.
- Background information on the topic: Only give enough background to provide a context; you may need to provide more background in the main body of the assignment.
- The question rephrased in your own words: Show that you understand the question by paraphrasing it.
- An indication of why the topic is important.
- A gap in previous research: Indicate what still needs to be addressed in a particular area, and where your research fits into the wider body of knowledge.

Unit 7 Conclusions

- Definitions of important words and terms: Only define the most important words, and do so briefly; further definition may need to be given in the main body.
- An indication of your subtopics: Tell your readers what smaller areas you will address in the main points.
- A thesis statement (which gives a plan of action for your assignment): Make clear to your readers what your main points will be and what perspective you will take. Usually the thesis statement comes at the end of the introduction. It can be one or two sentences.

The conclusion does not need to repeat any background from the introduction. Some people make the mistake of cutting and pasting the points from their introduction. This is inappropriate for two reasons: First, it is self-plagiarism; second, readers already know what you have told them in the introduction, so there is no need to repeat it. In particular, be careful to avoid telling your readers how you wrote the essay. They do not need to know: "This essay has considered a, b, and c. It has shown p, q, and r. It has also been claimed that x, y, and z." If you write this way, you are focusing on your action in writing, rather than on the ideas of the essay. It would be better to say: "In conclusion, a, b, and c are clearly important"; or "P, q, and r are key to...However, x, y, and z are less central to the argument." Do not add new information to a conclusion. If something is important, put it in the body of the essay.

A conclusion starts with specific information and becomes more general. It may include several of the following components:

- A summary of the main points: Remind your readers what the main points were, but don't use the same wording as elsewhere in the essay.
- Your findings, if applicable: Re-emphasize what you discovered after researching for this essay.
- Your response to the question, together with possible solutions: Restate your main argument, if you had an argument; remind the readers of your suggested solutions to any problems raised in the essay.
- Remaining problems and questions: Indicate what still needs to be solved.
- Areas for future research: Give suggestions for future research which could

address the same problem.

- A strong final sentence that leaves the readers with an overall impression of your views on the topic: Link your opinion to the broader topic.

(Retrieved from "Introductions and Conclusions" on the University of Adelaide website.)

 Questions:

1. Why is cutting and pasting the points from the introduction considered to be a mistake in writing the conclusion?
2. How is the conclusion related to the introduction?
3. In the introduction, it is usually considered the norm to identify the gap in previous research; in the conclusion, it is also a common practice to give suggestions for future research. In your opinion, how do these practices contribute to scholarly conversation?

Part IV
Reading for Speaking

The following two passages are the conclusions of two research papers in different fields. Read the passages and discuss the questions in groups to understand the content, wording, style, and structure of each conclusion.

Passage A

The current study extends the scope of motion research by examining how Cantonese-English-Japanese multilinguals lexicalize and conceptualize caused motion in a boundary-crossing situation. Specifically, it explores how language-specific patterns in lexicalization affect different levels of cognitive processing by using two types of measurements: a categorical measurement of similarity judgments and a continuous measurement of reaction time. Findings showed that in event lexicalization, multilingual speakers demonstrated a clear trend towards the target language in encoding path in the main verbs whereas manner in subordination when describing a boundary-crossing event. Although no cross-linguistic differences were found in the categorical preferences of event categorization, reaction time illustrated that multilingual speakers presented an ongoing process of cognitive restructuring towards the L3 in reacting much quicker to path-match alternate than manner-match alternate. In both tasks, the amount of language contact with L2 and L3 served as main predictors for the degree of cognitive restructuring for multilingual speakers.

The current findings demonstrate that learning an additional language may continue shaping or influencing bi- and multilingual's cognitive processing when the target language is actively involved in the decision-making process. In other words, learners are able to acquire relevant structures of the target language and corresponding thinking patterns when provided with sufficient language-specific instances (Athanasopoulos et al., 2015b; Bylund & Athanasopoulos, 2014a; Cadierno, 2010; Park, 2019). On the whole, the current findings show that learning a new language means acquiring an alternative way of thinking, and speakers can switch between distinct sets of thinking patterns depending on which language they are using. This new finding makes a timely contribution to the hypothesis of thinking-for-speaking, and sheds light on the complexity and diversity of how language shapes thought in the multilingual mind. This helps in understanding how people learn multiple languages.

Future research may combine the measurement of reaction time with the use of the eye-tracking technique to explore participants' attention allocation patterns during event perception. Also, other extra-linguistic factors such as language proficiency and length of immersion, need to be taken into further consideration when examining the dynamic relationship between the progress of language learning and change of cognitive state in the bi- or multilingual mind.

(Adapted from "Cognitive Restructuring in the Multilingual Mind: Language-specific Effects on Processing Efficiency of Caused Motion Events in Cantonese-English-Japanese Speakers" by Y. Wang & W. Li in *Bilingualism: Language and Cognition*, *11*(4) 2021.)

 **Questions:**

1. Do you think this is a good conclusion? Why or why not?

2. Based on your understanding of Passage B in Part Ⅲ, can you identify the components of this conclusion?

3. What signal phrases are used in this excerpt?

Passage B

Contributing to this special issue's investigations of the intersections of place and power, this article has drawn on the history and contemporary articulations of Manchester Chinatown to explore the temporal and the spatial dynamics of urban regeneration. Examining the intersection of place and time in the dominant narratives of Manchester Chinatown, I have sought to query spatial assumptions prevalent in existing analyses of the Chinese migrant interactions with the city. In so doing, the article has stressed the importance of emphasizing a relational interplay between time and space, where places are produced through "multiple becoming of space" and where temporality is "integral to the spatial" (Massey, 2005, pp.148+180). In particular, the article has challenged cultural delimitations of Chinatown as an "ethnic enclave" and considered the consequences of these practices of spatialization and temporalization for the area and the organizations associated with it. I have argued that the prevalent view of Chinatown as an ethnically defined space has served to exclude local Chinese organizations from further regeneration plans for the area. At the same time, prompted by the invasive forces of current city redevelopment and their entrapment in fixed notions of Chineseness, key organizations have left Chinatown. Their new locations around the city have prompted them to reconsider their public image and rearticulate their activities away from essential understandings of ethnicity and in relation to new constituencies. Yet, they remain trapped in the language of this ethnic urban area. The inability to recognize the interwoven complex history of Chinatown and the multiethnic nature of businesses and the workforce there can be gleaned from the marketing strategy of the Chinese New Year as the only niche for Chinatown in Manchester's redevelopment.

Rethinking the dimension of time as a means of seeing place and power has revealed the multilayered temporality/spatiality of the Manchester Chinese community situated within the larger ongoing forces of urban regeneration. Rather than viewing Chinatown as a space associated with a particular ethnic group—a perspective that locks both people and space within a particular national imaginary and nation time—it might be more productive to view it as an open space shaped by multiple historical and current trajectories.

The challenge is to view Chinatown as a recurrent social process. It is, in Bhabha's expression, a "disjunctive space" where "cultural interpretation" takes various forms (Bhabha, 1990, p.312). Or, in Massey's words, it is part of the process of contestation and negotiation in which the "constituent identities are also themselves continually moulded" (Massey, 2005, p.154). To recognize the interplay of spatial and temporal factors in the articulations of Chinatown would make it possible to acknowledge the complexities and intricacies of space-making and community-making, where both time and space are intimately related.

(Adapted from "Seeing Beyond an 'Ethnic Enclave': The Time/Space of Manchester Chinatown" by E. Barabantseva in *Identities*, *23*(1), 2016.)

 Questions:

1. Can you identify the components of this conclusion? How is it different from the one in Passage A above?

2. These two conclusions both start with a summary of the research questions. What do the two summaries have in common in terms of language and length?

3. What signal phrases are used in this excerpt?

Part V
Reading for Writing

Read the following conclusion and rewrite it with the expressions and strategies you have learned from this unit. Make sure you include the elements that have been marked in boldface below.

Summary of arguments [It can be seen, then, that chocolate is a right, as well as a social construct, but that different social groups within Australian higher education view the concept of "chocolate" differently. Lecturers tend to prefer dark chocolate, while students indicate a preference for milk chocolate, even though both types of chocolate are available.] **Area for future research** [More research is needed, however, to investigate gender and age differences in regard to these preferences.] **Remaining problems** [Worldwide, it is evident from the literature that despite greater transportability and increased production, in many locations chocolate is still only available to the privileged few. What is clear, therefore, is that although all should have a right to chocolate, this is not the case in every society, and even those who have this right do not always choose to exercise it.] **Strong final sentence** [Only when chocolate is finally available to everyone will it be possible to claim that chocolate is no longer restricted to the wealthy, but has become a right for every individual throughout the world.]

(Retrieved from "Introductions and Conclusions" on the University of Adelaide website.)

Exercises

I. Read the following conclusion taken from a student's research paper and improve it in terms of wording, style, and structure.

> The current study was about students' preferences towards written corrective feedback (WCF) with regard to WCF types and categories and compared their preferences with their teachers' beliefs and practices. Firstly, the importance of WCF was believed by both students and teachers. In terms of the WCF categories, it seemed safely to conclude that teachers' beliefs corresponded their students' perceptions. However, when it comes to which error category should be given priority to, I found that teachers' actual practices were somehow not in line with not only their self-assessments, but also students' preferences.
>
> Based on the comparison, firstly, I want to recommend that teachers should take students' preferences and reactions to different WCF types and categories into account when they are giving WCF in order to exaggerate the effectiveness of this activity. In addition, teacher trainings can be adopted to equip them with a guideline of how to give WCF.
>
> This study might make lots of potential contributions to the field. For other scholars, it is recommended to take student differences into account by evaluating different individuals' perceptions according to their second foreign language proficiency and motivation levels.

II. Read the following conclusion and then complete the tasks.

> In this paper I have discussed the question of social theory in food studies. First, I have highlighted how this question **has been scarcely explored** in this field, while **a great deal has been written about** the history, development, and state of the art of food studies. Based on Alan Warde's critique (2016) of a supposed lack of theoretical ambitions in food studies, I then claimed that food studies should seek

129

deeper engagements with social theories. By being more clearly engaged in social-theoretical debates, our diversities and theoretical conflicts will be more visible and, I **contend**, our explanations of food issues more sophisticated. Following this, I presented contemporary theories of practice, based on **a central distinction** between the extraordinary, deliberate, and expressive—the communicative functions that I have argued to **lie at the core of** food studies—and the everyday, unreflective, and routinized. By **engaging with** contemporary theories of practice, food consumption would be understood more in terms of everyday doings and social conventions, collectively routinized activities, embodied competences, shared and practical understandings, procedures, and sociomaterial relationships. I am not suggesting this to be the only, or even the "best" way forward; practice theories are and must **be subject to** criticism just like all theoretical traditions. However, **in line with** my plea to theoretical commitment, this is what I committed to myself.

Moreover, while my examples focus on consumption, practice-based food studies will also need to connect consumption to relations of production (e.g. Bååth, 2018). Shove, Pantzar, & Watson (2012) have argued that practices must be analyzed as tied to each other in bundles and nexuses. One such nexus could be to follow a certain food product from production to consumption, a classic example being Sidney Mintz's brilliant analysis of sugar in Western history (1986). As such, the researcher would follow "the social life of the thing" (Appadurai, 1986) and see how it becomes routinely used, ascribed meaning, how its materiality becomes a nodal point in the organization of everyday life, how competences develop around it, and more. As argued above, referring to Watson (2016), practice-based approaches to food issues must also highlight relations of power. Practices are stratified based on the concentrations of social status, financial resources, and power. Internally, individual participants and groups of participants are also stratified, for example, through divisions of labor and status in the practice of cooking (who performs the daily domestic cooking and who becomes a publicly celebrated chef?).

Food is an important part of the special as well as the mundane, the conspicuous, and the ordinary. It is a comparatively small empirical example, but the little things are, after all, what enables us to answer the big questions; it is through the ordinary that we understand the spectacular. This is the strength of food analysis, and I hope

Unit 7 Conclusions

in the future that food studies will become more theoretically engaged and thus more clearly divided into theoretical traditions and approaches. This will be an important advancement in a field that is developing quickly, and with great promise.

(Adapted from "On the Engagement with Social Theory in Food Studies: Cultural Symbols and Social Practices" by N. Neuman in *Food, Culture & Society*, 22(1), 2019.)

1. **Fill in the blanks with the bold-faced expressions in the text above. Change the form where necessary.**

   (1) Wage increases must be _____ inflation.

   (2) Recognition of patterns and inference skills _____ human learning.

   (3) Flights _____ delay because of the fog.

   (4) While the impact of display type has been studied for different kinds of tasks, it _____ in procedural training.

   (5) The local government needs to _____ local communities for better communication.

   (6) It is our client's _____ that the fire was an accident.

   (7) _____ Ernest Hemingway's distinctive style.

   (8) Philosophers did not use to make _____ between arts and science.

2. **Answer the following questions.**

   (1) In the conclusion, which part gives suggestions for future research?

   (2) A good conclusion often leaves the readers something to remember. What is the takeaway message of this article?

   (3) It is often suggested to avoid the first person pronoun "I" in academic writing in order to achieve an objective tone, but it is sometimes used by experienced writers or established scholars. In your opinion, what effect would the presence of "I" have on the readers?

III. Read the following sentences taken from the introduction and conclusion of the same paper. Separate them into two groups, Introduction and Conclusion, and put them in the right order to form a meaningful narrative.

(1) Despite these problems, it is possible for teachers to make a positive contribution to learners' knowledge in this important area.

(2) The essay which follows gives a brief history of relevant theory and discusses two major teaching strategies from a cognitive linguistic perspective.

(3) The concept of definiteness in relation to articles remains, however, more problematic, and needs further investigation.

(4) The evidence presented here suggests that learners do not use articles randomly, but that they choose articles according to whether or not the noun is countable.

(5) These small connecting words do not necessarily exist in other languages, or may not have exactly the same meanings.

(6) The use of articles in English has always been problematic for language learners.

(7) In conclusion, it is apparent that the most effective element in teaching of English articles is the reinforcement of the notion of countability.

(8) This makes teaching of this area very difficult, and research (Brala, 2002; Lindstromberg, 1998) indicates that no single method has yet proved successful.

(Retrieved from University of Adelaide website.)

Introduction: _____

Conclusion: _____

IV. Read the following conclusion excerpted from a journal article. Pay attention to the bold-faced expressions, and analyze the text to understand the function and structure of a typical conclusion in an academic article. Match each paragraph with the most appropriate description below the text.

① **This article has sought to** apply a form of embodied reflexivity to the research process. **This has allowed me to** analyze aspects of my research practice that may have otherwise been **overlooked** or taken for granted. An embodied perspective has **facilitated a fundamental analysis of** the relationship between researcher and research participants, researcher and research setting, and researcher and **the substantive focus of the study**.

② However, for the significance of the body, both as a physical entity and an organizing concept for the research, to be fully realized, **it needs to be seen within contemporary concerns about** childhood and the perceived risks associated with it. Current concerns about stranger danger, child abduction, and pedophilia are in many respects concerns about the violation of children's bodies. Moreover, children and childhood may be seen to embody an innocence and purity (Ennew, 1986) that **extends beyond** the individual child to represent childhood as a whole. Threats or violation of an individual child therefore **become symbolic of** violation of childhood per se. For example, media portrayals of Sarah Payne, and more recently Holly Wells and Jessica Chapman at the time of their abduction and dreadful murders, have imbued them with an almost mystical quality, as angelic bodies (golden curls, healthy sun tans, smiling faces, gingham check school uniform), pictures of innocence, to which many parents can relate. They have, therefore, come to represent (female) children more generally. Violation of these bodies has become symbolic of a violation of childhood and innocence themselves. As Mason & Falloon (2001) argue, child protection is based on a socialization paradigm in which concern is expressed not merely for the child as he or she exists but also for what he or she might become. It is, then, a concern not just for the future of the individual child but for all our futures.

③ The application of an embodied perspective to our methodology inevitably **brings these issues closer**. In particular, as ethnographers, working with, rather than on, children and their lives, we seek a degree of intimacy that is not available to other kinds of researchers. However, in doing so, **it is imperative that we recognize the need to** protect the children with whom we work and respect their right to privacy and anonymity. By the simple fact that we are there and are involved, this intimacy is an embodied intimacy. When those with whom we work, such as children, may be seen as vulnerable, then such intimacy may pose a threat to that vulnerability.

④ If this is the case, rather than bringing researcher and child closer together, child-centered methods may actually **result in** the construction of constraints and boundaries between researcher and child.

⑤ For those of us committed to the intimacy afforded by child-focused research methods and their capacity to allow us **a glimpse of** the interior world of the child, there is a need not only for an embodied reflexivity, but also for an embodied transparency in our work. This means that while we will not shirk sensitive subjects or look for corporeal distance behind more remote methods, we will be constantly aware not only of the possibilities offered by child-centered methods, but also of the difficulties they might pose to researchers and to children.

(Adapted from *Writing for Peer Reviewed Journals* by P. Thompson & B. Kamler in 2013.)

A. Implications for the field

B. Summary of what the article sets out to do and the benefits of the analysis

C. Reiteration of the necessity of an embodied perspective to ethnography

D. Concluding statements about a potential resolution

E. Claim for the timely significance of the article by elaborating on the child protection policy with strong emphasis on contemporary concerns

Para. 1 _____ Para. 2 _____ Para. 3 _____

Para. 4 _____ Para. 5 _____

Project

Work in groups. Collect ten conclusions from the journal articles in two different disciplines of humanities and social sciences. You need to perform the following tasks: analyze the structures and components of the conclusions; identify the signal phrases for each component; demonstrate the differences in conclusion composition between the two disciplines (if any), in terms of wording, style, and structure; and finally report the group work in class.

Unit 8

Reviewers' Comments and Editors' Decisions

Part I
Introducing the Unit

In this unit, we are going to learn how to read reviewers' comments and editors' decisions. In the publication process, most journals require a blind review of manuscripts by multiple (usually two or three) anonymous experts in the field. This peer review system is designed to provide an unbiased and thorough assessment of the submitted article to assist editors in decision-making about the manuscript.

Reviewers' comments point out the strengths and weaknesses of the article and often offer professional suggestions for improvement, but the comments can vary in length and style. Editors base their decisions not only on the reviewers' reports but also on their own reading of the manuscript. For instance, before the article is sent for blind review, the editors will consider whether it falls within the scope of the journal and whether it meets the required standard. Editorial decisions usually fall into the main categories of acceptance, revision and rejection. Learning how to read and understand reviewers' comments and editors' decisions is crucial to successful publication.

In the following parts, we will discuss different kinds of feedback that writers typically receive from journals, explore the ways to decode reviewer reports, present the strategies for approaching the revise and resubmit process, and illustrate the techniques in writing back to editors.

After finishing this unit, you are expected to achieve the following learning objectives:

- to demonstrate familiarity with typical types of editor decision letters;
- to decode and prioritize reviewers' comments correctly;
- to respond to reviewers' comments and editors' decisions using appropriate format and language;
- to comprehend the reasons for negative feedback;
- to understand manuscript status in online submission systems;
- to deal with negative emotions that might occur in the publication process calmly and take it as a good opportunity to engage with the discourse community.

Unit 8 Reviewers' Comments and Editors' Decisions

Part II
Reading for Expressions

Study the bold-faced expressions that are often used in reviewers' comments and editors' decisions, or in response letters to them.

A. Reviewers' Comments

- **The main strengths of this paper are that** it **addresses** an interesting and timely question, finds a **novel** solution based on a carefully selected set of rules, and provides a clear answer.
- **The weakness of this paper is** the not always easy **readability** of the text which establishes unclear logical links between concepts.
- The article is **well-constructed**, the experiments were **well-conducted**, and the analysis was **well-performed**.
- This means the strong conclusions **put forward by** this manuscript are not **warranted** and I cannot approve the manuscript **in this form**.
- I think this paper is excellent and **an important addition to the literature**.
- The paper would be both more **compelling** and useful to **a broad readership** if it suggests a way forward.
- It may **be beyond the scope of** this paper to **fully examine** incentive structures.
- The **takeaway message** of this paper should **be more explicitly stated**.
- Young's theory should **be acknowledged or credited** at least, if not actively **grappled with**.

B. Editors' Decisions

- **I am pleased to inform you that** *Language and Literature* would like to **publish your manuscript**.
- Following careful consideration by the journal's **editorial board** and **anonymous reviewers**, **I regret to inform you that** we are unable to **accept your submission**.
- I am **attaching a document** with some basic required **edits** that need to be applied to your manuscript before it's published.
- You will also receive **a proof of your manuscript** for final review.
- In order to **proceed to** publish your submission, we will need you to submit

137

the following documents.

- We're excited to **move forward with** your submission.
- Please **revise** the paper according to the reviewers' comments and **resubmit** before the deadline for timely publication.
- We **evaluate** all manuscript submissions as **expeditiously** as possible and appreciate your patience throughout the **peer review** process.
- At this point, your manuscript **has been assigned to** an editor and **is awaiting** reviewer confirmations.
- Your manuscript **is under external review** with 1 of 3 required reviews submitted.
- Your manuscript has all external reviews submitted and is awaiting **final editorial review**.

C. Responses to Reviewers' Comments and Editors' Decisions

- We **are grateful to** the editors and reviewers for their time and **constructive/ insightful/valuable comments** on our manuscript.
- Thanks for **raising these important points / pointing this out / bringing this point to our attention**.
- We agree with this and have **incorporated** your suggestion throughout the manuscript.
- We have, accordingly, **revised/changed/modified** the second part to emphasize this point.
- Thank you for this suggestion. It would have been interesting to explore this aspect. However, in the case of our study, **it seems slightly out of scope**.
- I have **implemented** their comments and suggestions and wish to submit a revised version of the manuscript **for further consideration** in the journal.
- The following is **a point-by-point/section-by-section response** explaining how we have **addressed** each of the editors' or reviewers' comments.
- Changes in the **initial** version of the manuscript are either **highlighted** for added sentences or **strikethrough** for deleted sentences in the revised version.
- We **look forward to the outcome of your assessment**.
- We will **respond to any further questions** on our submissions or revisions.
- We look forward to hearing from you **in due time**.

Unit 8 Reviewers' Comments and Editors' Decisions

Part III
Reading for Ideas

The following two passages discuss the categories of typical editor decision letters and the reasons for negative reviewer feedback respectively. Read the passages and answer the questions to understand the main ideas of each passage.

Passage A

Sending an article to a journal to be reviewed is not simply acquiring two or three readers. Referees are trusted members of the discourse community that read and support the journal. They have been selected because they know and can speak for the more general readership: They also have expertise about topics related to the article, may have published in the same area, or may even appear in the article's reference list. Some journals, *The British Journal of Sociology of Education* for example, only use their editorial boards as reviewers, making the review process a much more consistent expression of a particular "take" on a field. Most journals, however, have a database of reviewers to call on. The vast majority of editors now report that it is harder to get people to review and that they often have to cast the net wider than might be desirable or to call on the same people over and over again. It is the wide-net approach that is generally responsible for widely divergent and often conflicting reviews.

All journals use reviewer pro formas which typically ask for a global recommendation: acceptance, minor revisions, major revisions, or rejection. Reviewers are also sometimes offered categories of response about the fit with the journal, the structure of the article, and the quality of the writing. There is always space provided for reviewers to make additional comments to the author and, sometimes, confidential comments to the editor. Editors often provide specific guidance on the tone of these comments, suggesting that reviewers focus on the positive and offer concrete suggestions for changes, rather than vague homilies. Despite this scaffolding, what reviewers actually write in the space for comments varies enormously.

When writers receive comments back from the editor, with reviewer comments attached, they are not simply being told what revisions to make. They are now in an asynchronous conversation with the discourse community. The writer has sent the discourse community something and they have responded. And the editor is a powerful arbiter of this conversation.

It is relatively uncommon to receive unconditional acceptance from the reviewing process. Any of the other three options—major and minor revisions, and rejection—are the most likely. Minor revisions are, or ought to be, a cause for celebration. We want to examine the last two possible fates of the journal article in more detail: rejection, and revise and resubmit, since these are the most difficult to handle. The following outlines the ways in which reviewer recommendations are actioned:

- Unconditional acceptance: These articles are forwarded to the editor who will then send them to the publisher to be copy-edited.
- Accept with minor revisions: The editor will forward a copy of the referees' reports to the author with a request that the revisions be made. The author should then return the revised article to the editor; it then goes to the publisher for copy-editing.
- Revise and resubmit: The editor will forward a copy of the referees' reports to the author invited to resubmit the article after it has been revised to take into account the comments made in the referees' evaluation reports. Once resubmitted it will most often be returned to the original referees for their assessment.
- Reject: The editor will return the submission and the referees' reports to the author, who will not be invited to resubmit the article.

(Adapted from *Writing for Peer Reviewed Journals* by P. Thompson & B. Kamler in 2013.)

 Questions:

1. Why are referees invited to review the articles submitted to a journal?

2. According to the excerpt, writers are in an asynchronous conversation with the discourse community when they receive comments back from editors. What is your understanding of this statement?

3. What are the differences between "accept with minor revisions" and "revise and resubmit"?

Unit 8 Reviewers' Comments and Editors' Decisions

Passage B

Journal editors and reviewers are unconcerned with the emotional roller coaster you may be riding as you struggle to keep from being completely demoralized by suggestions for rewriting your piece. What they are concerned with is how you respond to their requests to reshape and revise the manuscript. As you consider next steps, there are several tasks you need to undertake, the first of which is to determine the reasons for any negative feedback you have received. Once you know the cause of the criticisms, you are much better placed to address them.

In some ways, the easiest feedback to receive is that your piece does not fall within the journal's scope. As a reviewer for adult education journals on three continents, I am often struck by how many pieces I review that either do not mention adult learning or adult education at all or provide a cursory sentence or two tacked on to the opening and closing paragraphs while the bulk of the article resolutely steers clear of any other mentions. If you have submitted an article to a journal without convincing yourself and convincing the reader that your work is clearly within the journal's scope of interest, it should be no surprise to get feedback requiring you to demonstrate the relevance of your work for the journal's readership.

At other times it may be the form of your work, rather than its content, that is the problem. Placing a piece of qualitative research in a journal that features only statistical or experimental research is clearly pointless. Likewise, exceeding the page limit because of your attraction to long, verbatim extracts from your research will often disqualify you. Some journals have a house policy of no first-person writing, in which case an autoethnography is clearly going to receive negative feedback. Authors also sometimes create needless problems for themselves by using a citation style different from the one specified by the journal. All of these things indicate to a reviewer that you have not bothered to read the guidelines for contributors that most journals reprint in every issue, and they call your scholarly credibility into question.

More difficult are situations in which your piece has run into opposition that is more ideological, such as an article that analyzes Queer Theory or Afrocentrism that is returned because the reviewers regard those perspectives as discredited or insufficiently intellectual. In my own case, I have spent several years trying to place a piece on how adults learn to deal with clinical depression, using myself as a case study, with no success. Many pieces are also returned because the intent of the article is unclear to the extent that it lacks even the most cursory statement of purpose. Despite my own success in eventually placing my own pieces in refereed journals, I still receive criticism to the effect that my purpose of writing an article is unclear. This is usually when I am so captivated by the topic that its inherent fascination seems to require no explicit elaboration.

More specific reasons for rejection are that an author has, in the opinion of the reviewers, misinterpreted or misunderstood central concepts, made false inferences from data, neglected to include relevant research or theory that casts important light on the problem, made factual errors in wrongly attributing events or theories, omitted potential criticisms of the work outlined in the article, or simply reproduced work that is already published. These are more easily addressed than the most damning criticism of all in my opinion: that an author's writing is incomprehensible. Short of going to a remedial writing clinic and undertaking an intensive course in academic writing, there is little one can do in the face of that particular criticism. It is particularly demoralizing when it happens in a field that prizes clarity of communication as one of the highest of all scholarly virtues.

(Adapted from *The Handbook of Scholarly Writing and Publishing* by T. S. Rocco & T. Hatcher in 2011.)

 Questions:

1. What are the reasons for negative feedback as given in the excerpt?

2. What are the suggestions provided by the authors to reduce the possibility of receiving negative feedback? What else can writers do?

3. How do you deal with the negative emotions that might occur in the publication process?

Unit 8　Reviewers' Comments and Editors' Decisions

Part IV
Reading for Speaking

The following two passages discuss how to respond to reviewers' feedback and what typical editor decision letters look like respectively. Read the passages and discuss the questions in groups to learn to prioritize reviewers' comments and understand the categories and formats of editor decision letters.

Passage A

　　Probably the first technical task facing an author receiving negative feedback is to try to prioritize the kinds of comments received. It is important to remember that not all editorial suggestions are requirements; some are just what they say: suggestions. So at the outset, try to sort out which parts of reviewers' comments are non-negotiable and absolutely required and which fall more into the category of "it would also be nice if…". Along with this task is the prioritizing of which parts of reviewers' comments to address first. In my opinion, the initial strategy should be to decide which comments are big picture comments—those that deal with the structure of the piece and call for major structural reorganization. For example, if a reviewer writes that your literature review should be drastically reduced or that a small section of the first draft should comprise the focal point of a resubmitted draft, then addressing those issues is the first order of business. I have often received feedback that has isolated one part of my work and asked me to develop it more fully, while deleting or significantly reducing much of the original paper. This is usually because the reviewer shows me where material I am elaborating on at length has already been published and which other parts of the piece explore ideas not previously documented. This kind of analysis is extremely helpful and ensures that your article has a better chance of being accepted and of having a wider impact in the field. So the first priority is to sort out the structural advice and decide how that is going to be addressed.

　　After the big picture, first-order, structural changes come the more detailed second-order comments. These are much more specific, having to do with subheads that need to be inserted, research that needs to be acknowledged, ideas that need to be developed or explained more fully, criticisms that need to be dealt with, contradictions that remain unrecognized, and so on. The list of specific suggestions and requests is much more likely to contain items that fit the "it would be nice to address this if you have space" category, so here you have to judge which of these should receive your attention. Sometimes you will be in the situation where one section or point that one reviewer finds problematic is lauded by another reviewer. In those situations, you can usually use much more discretion in deciding whether to respond to them. As a general rule, if more than one reviewer makes the same observation or criticism, that is a good reason for attending to it in the second draft. If the editors are doing their job properly, they will prioritize the reviewers' comments in a cover letter that sets out what is expected of you for the second draft. But sometimes editors are so overwhelmed by fitting their editorial duties into an already crowded life that they simply give you the verdict of revising and resubmitting, together with copies of the different reviewers' comments.

When deciding which parts of reviewers' comments to address first, it is often helpful to have colleagues to bounce ideas off. We are sometimes so close to our own work that changing one word, or deleting one sentence, seems to rip out a piece of our soul. In my own case, if I have labored long and hard over a paragraph or a page, if I am enormously proud of what seems to me to be a wonderfully lyrical passage, or if I have spent weeks reading and then distilling a massive amount of work into a page or two, the suggestion from a reviewer that these things be deleted is very hard to take. But it is a major mistake to assume that the length or intensity of one's effort as a writer is correlated with its perceived relevance or usefulness to a reader. I have often written articles that have required months of reading and analysis to make sure I have understood the gist of a theory correctly, only to find that the section on implications for practice that I dashed off as an afterthought, and that was based on a quick review of my experience, is the one a journal reviewer selects as the most significant aspect of the whole article. If you can call on a colleague or two to do a quick read of your article, and if they agree with the substance of the reviewers' comments, this helps you force yourself to deal with those comments. A colleague can also help you focus on which elements of the reviewers' comments he or she feels you should take most seriously.

(Adapted from *The Handbook of Scholarly Writing and Publishing* by T. S. Rocco & T. Hatcher in 2011.)

Unit 8   Reviewers' Comments and Editors' Decisions

 Questions:

1. What is the first thing to do when an author receives negative feedback?

2. What are big picture or first-order comments? What are second-order comments? Please give examples for each category.

3. When you are deciding which parts of reviewers' comments to address first, why is it helpful to turn to a colleague?

Passage B

After initial editorial screening or receiving all the required reviewers' reports, journal editors will usually make the first decision on the submitted manuscript in a timely manner. Editor decision letters usually follow certain formats and the following are four typical templates that demonstrate the formats and language used for different decisions.

Manuscript Acceptance Letter

> Dear [Author name],
>
> I am pleased to inform you that your manuscript "[Manuscript title]" is accepted for publication in [Journal name, italicized]. I am attaching a document with some basic required edits that need to be applied to your manuscript before it's published.
>
> In order to proceed to publish your submission, we will need you to submit the following:
>
> - A signed author agreement: [Add link here];
> - Your edited manuscript—please include all of the edits outlined in the attached file;
> - [Insert any additional items that the journal requires here].
>
> At this time we also want to remind you of our copyright and open access policies, [Add link here]. Once your manuscript is moved to publishing, our production editor will keep you informed of your article's progress in the production process. You will also receive a proof of your manuscript for final review.

We're excited to move forward with your submission. Please feel free to e-mail me with any questions.

Sincerely,

[Editor name]

Revise and Resubmit Request

Dear [Author name],

Thank you for submitting your manuscript "[Manuscript title]" to [Journal name, italicized]. The editorial team and a group of expert reviewers have assessed your submission and feel that it has potential for publication, and so we would like to invite you to revise the paper and resubmit for further review.

We appreciate that your paper addresses [Positive quality about the paper's key objective], but there were some concerns raised with regard to [Key concerns]. Please see the attached reviewer comments for further details about necessary revisions.

We ask that you submit the revised version of your manuscript by [Explanation of how to do this]. Please note, your revised manuscript should be accompanied by a summary of your responses to the reviewers' comments.

You have [Number] weeks to respond to this revise and resubmit request ending on [Deadline], after which point we will presume that you have withdrawn your submission from [Journal name, italicized].

Please feel free to contact me with any questions.

Sincerely,

[Editor name]

Unit 8   Reviewers' Comments and Editors' Decisions

Desk Rejection

Dear [Author name],

Thank you for submitting your manuscript "[Manuscript title]" to [Journal name, italicized]. After careful consideration by our editors, we regret to inform you that we must decline this submission on editorial grounds and subsequently have declined to send the paper out to external peer reviewers. We found that [Explanation of why this particular manuscript is not fit for the publication]. This paper may be a better fit for [Name(s) of other journals, italicized].

We thank you for your interest, and hope you choose to submit another article for review in the future.

Sincerely,

[Editor name]

Manuscript Rejection Letter Following Peer Review

Dear [Author name],

Thank you for submitting your manuscript "[Manuscript title]" to [Journal name, italicized]. Following careful consideration by the journal's editorial board and expert reviewers, I regret to inform you that we are unable to accept your submission.

Although [Positive qualities about the manuscript], our editorial board and expert reviewers determined that the paper [Explanation of why the paper doesn't meet the publication standards of the journal]. Primary concerns expressed were that: [Specific concerns].

I am including the reviewers' comments in this e-mail for your reference. I hope you find this information helpful for submission to another journal, and we hope to see more of your work in the future.

Sincerely,

[Editor name]

(Retrieved from "7 E-mail Templates for Common Peer Review Correspondences" on Scholastica website.)

 Questions:

1. Do you find any new or difficult words or expressions? Discuss them with your group members.

2. What do you need to do after receiving the "manuscript acceptance letter" and the "revise and resubmit request" respectively?

3. Interview your supervisor or any other teacher about whether he or she has ever received any of the above editor decision letters. Share his or her experiences with your group members.

4. Apart from the four most common situations mentioned above, are there any other scenarios where you might need to contact the editors according to your interview?

Part V
Reading for Writing

Read the following two templates for responding to reviewers' comments. Familiarize yourself with the format and mark the expressions that you find useful. Based on your knowledge of typical editor decision letters and reviewers' comments, first write an editor decision letter in the tone of a journal editor and then write a response letter to it in the tone of the writer. Please follow the template format and use the expressions learned from this unit wherever possible.

Unit 8 Reviewers' Comments and Editors' Decisions

Template 1—General Template

Dear Prof./Dr./ Mr./Ms. [Editor name],

Thank you for giving me/us the opportunity to submit a revised draft of my/our manuscript titled [Manuscript title] to [Journal name]. I/We appreciate the time and effort that you and the reviewers have dedicated to providing your valuable feedback on my/our manuscript. I am / We are grateful to the reviewers for their insightful comments. I/We have been able to incorporate changes to reflect most of the suggestions provided by the reviewers. I/We have highlighted the changes within the manuscript.

Here is a point-by-point response to the reviewers' comments and concerns.

Comments from Reviewer 1

[How to respond to comments that you agree with]

- Comment 1: [Paste the full comment here.]
  Response: [Type your response here.] Thank you for pointing this out. I/We agree with this comment. Therefore, I/we have…[Explain what change you have made. Mention exactly where in the revised manuscript this change can be found—page number, paragraph, and line.]

- Comment 2: [Paste the full comment here.]
  Response: Agree. I/We have, accordingly, done/revised/changed/modified… to emphasize this point. [Discuss the change made, providing the necessary explanation/clarification. Mention exactly where in the revised manuscript this change can be found—page number, paragraph, and line.]

- Comment 3: [Paste the full comment here.]
  Response: I/We agree with this and have incorporated your suggestion throughout the manuscript.

[How to respond to comments that you disagree with]

- Comment 1: [Paste the full comment here.]
  Response: [Type your response here.] Thank you for this suggestion. It would have been interesting to explore this aspect. However, in the case of my/our

study, it seems slightly out of scope because…[Provide a clear explanation/ justification with supporting evidence as far as possible.]

- Comment 2: [Paste the full comment here.]
  Response: [Type your response here.] You have raised an important point here. However, I/we believe that…would be more appropriate because…[Provide your justification with clear reasoning/supporting evidence.]

Comments from Reviewer 2

- Comment 1: [Paste the full comment here.]
  Response: [Follow the patterns recommended above.]

Additional Clarifications

[Here, mention any other clarifications you would like to provide for the journal editor/reviewers.]

In addition to the above comments, all spelling and grammatical errors pointed out by the reviewers have been corrected.

I/We look forward to hearing from you in due time regarding my/our submission and to responding to any further questions and comments you may have.

Sincerely,

[Corresponding author name]

Template 2—Responses by Section

Dear Prof./Dr./ Mr./Ms. [Editor name],

I/We would like to express my/our heartfelt thanks to the reviewers for their insightful comments. I/We have carefully read their comments, which are extremely useful for expanding the main arguments of the article. I/We have made the revisions according to the reviewers' comments and highlighted the changes within the manuscript. The following is a section-by-section response to the reviewers' comments.

Unit 8 Reviewers' Comments and Editors' Decisions

ABSTRACT

Comments from Reviewer 1

- Comment 1: [Paste the full comment here.]

    Response: [Follow the patterns recommended above.]

Comments from Reviewer 2

- Comment 1: [Paste the full comment here.]

    Response: [Follow the patterns recommended above.]

[List the other comments for this section in the same format.]

INTRODUCTION

Comments from Reviewer 1

- Comment 1: [Paste the full comment here.]

    Response: [Follow the patterns recommended above.]

Comments from Reviewer 2

- Comment 1: [Paste the full comment here.]

    Response: [Follow the patterns recommended above.]

[List the other comments for this section in the same format.]

[Continue this for the other sections in the manuscript.]

Additional Clarifications

[Here, mention any other clarifications you would like to provide for the journal editor/reviewers.]

I/We look forward to hearing from you soon.

Sincerely,

[Corresponding author name]

(Retrieved from "A Template for Responding to Peer Reviewer Comments" on Editage Insights website.)

Exercises

I. Read the following response letter to an editor's decision and improve it in terms of wording, style, and structure.

> Dear Editor,
>
> I am Ming Li. My manuscript is entitle "Impoliteness and Power Dynamics in Intimate Interactions in Short Stories". I made revisions point by point. The following is the list of responses to the suggestions in details. All the revised parts in the manuscript are labelled in red.
>
> Thank you very much again for your kind help.
>
> Best regards.
>
> Yours sincerely,
>
> Ming Li

II. Read the following passage and then complete the tasks.

> ### Responding to Manuscript Reviewer and Editor Comments
>
> (1) _____. The key objective of the peer review is to improve the quality of the manuscript. Thus, this should be viewed by the authors as an important professional service for their growth and development. The reviewers volunteer hours of their time in reviewing the manuscript and providing general and specific comments on the organization, clarity, rigor, and **validity** of the work and how to improve them. An appreciation of these facts may help authors in considering this as a necessary and important step in the review process rather than an obstacle in having their paper published.
>
> (2) _____. It is essential to have all authors review all comments and provide their responses for the primary author. Any negative or emotional reaction

to the reviewers and the editor who provide comments **critical** of a manuscript reflecting months and years of the authors' hard work should be avoided.

(3) _____. It is often necessary for all listed authors of a submission to meet in person or electronically to discuss all comments and possible next steps for their responses. The primary author should prepare a draft based on input from all authors for their return comments to remarks made by the reviewers and the editor. Again, all comments from the reviewers and the editor should be **addressed**.

(4) _____. The authors must decide how to respond in a thoughtful way to any requests for additional data, which may require further laboratory work or require the collection of more patient data. Authors must not give up or appear to resist making such changes, but rather respond with evidence and explanation to comments where they agree and disagree with the reviewers.

(5) _____. It is not uncommon where one reviewer may ask authors to add content in various sections (e.g., text, tables, figures, and references), whereas another may suggest a shortening of the manuscript. One may recommend converting text into a table or figure when the reverse may be suggested by another. These should be considered normal individual perspectives and not evoke frustration among authors. The authors as a group must decide what is the best presentation of their work for clarity and impact and then explain their decisions when responding to the reviewers' and the editor's comments. When continuing concerns about which direction manuscript revisions should take with regard to conflicting reviewer comments, the editor of the journal should be contacted for further direction.

(6) _____. Once the primary author has considered input from all co-authors for comments, the next step is to revise the manuscript with **track changes**. The revised manuscript with track changes should then be critically reviewed by all authors to make certain all comments have been addressed in the revised version. If needed, the authors can seek its review by other experts at or outside their institution as needed.

(7) _____. This is an important document, which should be prepared by the primary author with input from the co-authors to clearly indicate how each comment was addressed leading to the modified text and why certain comments did not require

changes in the revised manuscript. All reviewer comments should be addressed and **incorporated** into the manuscript unless any changes will negatively affect the quality of the submission; an explanation of any reviewer or editor comments not addressed should be provided. The document should be well organized, and the authors should be polite and respectful rather than defensive and confrontational, even if certain comments of the reviewers appear to be harsh or **unjustified**.

(8) _____. This letter should thank the editor for the peer review of the manuscript and highlight the importance and potential impact of the authors' work. Occasionally, an author may perceive a misunderstanding or an incomplete assessment of their manuscript by a certain reviewer. This should be indicated to the editor. In such cases, the editor may ask an additional reviewer to evaluate the manuscript **prior to** reaching a decision about its acceptance or rejection.

(9) _____. All authors must review and approve these final four documents: "Cover letter to the editor," "Responses to the editor and reviewers' comments," "Revised manuscript with track changes," and "**Clean copy** of the revised manuscript." When these documents have been completed, it is advisable to take a short break from them for a few hours or days to overcome fatigue and encourage a fresh subsequent look at the documents to capture additional deficiencies prior to submission.

(10) _____. It is an important step for the authors to determine where to go next if the revised manuscript is rejected despite the best efforts made by the authors during the revision process. Authors should not be so discouraged that they just give up and cease efforts in attempting to get their work published; delays in doing so can make the work appear old and less relevant.

(Adapted from "Responding to Manuscript Reviewer and Editor Comments" by M. C. Nahata & E. M. Sorkin in *Annals of Pharmacotherapy*, 53(9), 2019.)

1. Match each blank in the text with the most appropriate topic sentence below.

    A. Review each comment of the reviewers and the editor with an open and calm mind.

    B. Understand the importance of the peer review process.

Unit 8 Reviewers' Comments and Editors' Decisions

C. Review the entire packet of the thoroughly revised manuscript and then submit it.

D. Decide on how to address varying comments of the reviewers and the editor on the same issue.

E. Review each comment of the reviewers and the editor to identify possible responses.

F. Develop a plan of action for comments requiring additional work.

G. Prepare a letter to the editor explaining the potential impact of the work.

H. Know where to go if your manuscript is rejected.

I. Prepare a document "Responses to the editor and reviewers' comments" in a polite and respectful tone.

J. Revise the manuscript with track changes responding to all comments and have it critically reviewed.

2. **Fill in the blanks with the bold-faced expressions in the text above. Change the form where necessary.**

   (1) She had _____ reasons for not supporting the proposals.

   (2) Many of your suggestions have been _____ into the plan.

   (3) We must _____ ourselves to the problem of traffic pollution.

   (4) _____ is a piece of writing that doesn't need much work by an editor to make it ready for publication.

   (5) Her success _____ the faith her teachers has put in her.

   (6) _____ is useful in the editing process of a document, especially when you ask others for feedback.

   (7) This route would have enabled humans to enter southern areas of the Americas _____ the melting of the continental glaciers.

   (8) The company has been _____ for not taking the problem seriously.

III. Most journals use online submission systems, such as ScholarOne, Editorial Manager, and EVISE®. These submission systems provide authors, editors, and reviewers with an efficient and easy-to-access method of checking the status of a manuscript, and differ only slightly in terms and processing. Read the following guide to various stages that a manuscript undergoes post submission and then explain each stage in your own words.

Manuscript Status in Online Submission Systems

Manuscript Submitted: This means that the manuscript has been successfully submitted and approved by the author. After this, the manuscript usually goes through a formatting check by the journal staff before it is assigned to an editor.

Editor Invited: This step is optional and may not occur in all journals. This means that the manuscript has been assigned to an editor and is waiting for the editor's acceptance.

With Editor: This status indicates that an editor has taken charge of the manuscript. At this stage, the editor completes an initial screening of the manuscript, and if he/she finds it suitable for the journal, it is sent for peer review. If the manuscript does not match the scope of the journal or does not meet the standards of the journal, it will be returned without review. In such cases, it might show "Decision in Process" as the next status, and in all probability, the author will be informed of the rejection in a few days.

Reviewer Invited: This step is optional as it may not occur in all journals. Once a paper passes the initial screening stage, the editor looks for peer reviewers for the paper. When the system shows the status "Reviewer Invited", it means that invitations have been sent out to reviewers, but they have not yet accepted. Sometimes, the tracking system may show the "Reviewer Invited" status for some time and then move back to "With Editor", This probably means that the peer reviewers have declined the invitations, and the editor will now have to look for other reviewers.

Under Review: This status means that the manuscript is under peer review. Peer review is an honorary service that requires detailed scrutiny and evaluation of the manuscript. Hence, this is perhaps the most time-consuming part of the entire publication process. It can take anywhere between one to four months, depending on the journal and the field of study.

Required Reviews Complete: This status indicates that all the peer reviews have been completed and received by the editorial office. Sometimes, the editor, after going through the reviews, might feel that an additional review is required. In such cases, the status might go back to "Under Review". So, do not be surprised if this happens: Once the additional review is completed, the status will come back to "Required Reviews Complete".

Decision in Process: This means that the editor is now taking a decision on your paper based on the peer reviewer comments and his/her own opinion. If required, the editor may consult the editorial board at this stage. Once this status shows up, the author is generally informed of the editorial decision in a few days. However, in some exceptional situations, several weeks pass by with this status constantly being displayed, and the author does not receive any decision. This might happen if the editor is very busy and there are a lot of other papers queued up at his/her table, waiting for their turn.

Revise: This indicates that the author has been asked to make major or minor revisions depending on the reviewer comments, and the submission is now with the author. The author is usually given a deadline of a few weeks to a couple of months depending on the nature of revisions and the field of study. The author can request that the deadline be extended by writing to the editor in advance. The author needs to submit the revised manuscript along with a point-by-point response to the reviewer comments.

Revised Manuscript Submitted: This indicates that the author has submitted the revised document. The document is now awaiting a formatting check by the journal.

Author Declines to Revise: This shows that the author has clicked on an action link indicating that he/she does not wish to submit a revised version of the manuscript. In other words, the author is not ready to make the revisions suggested and would like to withdraw his/her paper.

Completed Withdrawal: If an author chooses to withdraw his/her paper, the withdrawal process is complete once the author has put in a request for withdrawal and the editor has agreed to it. Remember that an e-mail from the editor confirming the withdrawal is absolutely necessary before the manuscript can be submitted to another journal; else it may be considered as a duplicate or simultaneous submission.

Completed Reject: In case the author has made the revisions requested by the peer reviewers and the editor, the final decision on the manuscript could be either "accept" or "reject". In case the editor is not satisfied with the revisions, the paper could be rejected. This status shows that based on the revisions and the author's responses to the reviewer comments, the editor has made a final decision of rejecting the paper.

Completed Accept: This status indicates that the editor is satisfied with the revisions made by the author and has made a final decision of acceptance.

(Retrieved from "Tracking Your Manuscript Status in Journal Submission Systems" on Editage Insights website.)

IV. **Read the following peer review report. Pay attention to the bold-faced expressions. Based on the classification criteria of reviewers' comments set out in Passage A in Part IV, answer the questions.**

It is a **well-written**, needed, and useful summary of the current status of "data publication" from a certain perspective. ① The authors, however, need to be **bolder** and more **analytical**. This is an opinion piece, yet I see little opinion. A certain view is implied by the organization of the paper and the references chosen, but they could be more **explicit**.

② The paper would be both more **compelling** and useful to **a broad readership** if the authors moved beyond providing a simple summary of the landscape and examined why there is controversy in some areas and then use the evidence they have compiled to **suggest a path forward**. They need to be more **forthright** in saying what data publication means to them, or what parts of it they do not deal with. Are they satisfied with the Lawrence et al. definition? Do they accept the **critique** of Parsons and Fox? What is the **scope** of their essay?

③ The discussion of data citation was good and **captured the state of the art** well, but again I would have liked to see some views on a way forward. Have we solved the basic problem and are now just dealing with **edge cases**? Is the "just-in-time identifier" the way to go? What are the **implications**? Will the more basic solutions work **in the interim**?

Indeed there is little if any evidence that data publication and citation **incentivize** data sharing or stewardship. As Christine Borgman suggests, we need to look more closely at who we are trying to incentivize to do what. There is no reason to assume it follows the same model as research literature publication. ④ It may be **beyond the scope of** this paper to **fully examine** incentive structures, but it at least needs to be **acknowledged** that building on the current model doesn't seem to be working.

⑤ Finally, what is the **takeaway message** from this essay? It ends rather abruptly with no summary, no suggested directions or immediate challenges to overcome, no **call to action**, no **indications** of things we should stop trying, and only brief mention of alternative perspectives.

Overall, this is a timely and needed essay. It is **well researched** and **nicely written**. With **modifications** addressing the detailed comments below and better recognizing the complexity of the current data publication landscape, this will be a **worthwhile** review paper. With more significant modification where the authors **dig deeper into** the complexities and controversies and truly **grapple with** their implications to suggest a way forward, this could be a very **influential** paper.

Detailed Comments:

⑥ The whole paper needs a quick **copy-edit**. There are a few **typos**, missing words, and wrong verb tenses. Note the word "data" is a plural noun (e.g., Data are not software, nor are they literature).

⑦ Page 2, Para. 2: "Citability is addressed by assigning a PID." This is not true, as the authors discuss on Page 4, Para. 4.

⑧ Page 4, Para. 2: The joint declaration of data citation principles involved many more organizations than Force11, CODATA, and DCC. Please **credit** them all (maybe in a footnote).

⑨ Page 6, Para. 3: Parsons and Fox don't just argue that the data publication metaphor is limiting. They also say it is misleading. That should be acknowledged at least, if not actively grappled with.

(Retrieved from "Peer Review Examples" on F1000Research website.)

 Questions:

1. What is the tone of the reviewer? What do you think of the comments made in this review report?

2. Among the underlined comments, which are non-negotiable, i.e., requirements? Which fall more into the "it would be nice to address this if you have space" category, i.e., suggestions?

   Requirements: _____

   Suggestions: _____

3. Among the underlined comments, which can be put in the category of first-order comments? Which are the second-order comments?

   First-order comments: _____

   Second-order comments: _____

Project

Work in groups. Collect ten response letters to editors' decisions and reviewers' comments in two different disciplines of humanities and social sciences. You need to perform the following tasks: analyze the format and language of the letters; identify the organization and diction of the responses to reviewers' comments; summarize the strengths and weaknesses of the letters in terms of wording, style, and structure; demonstrate the differences in letter writing between the two disciplines (if any); and finally report the group work in class.

References

Barabantseva, E. (2016). Seeing beyond an "ethnic enclave": The time/space of Manchester Chinatown. *Identities*, *23*(1), 99–115.

Bhatia, V. K. (2013). *Analyzing Genre*. Boston: Addison-Wesley.

Boluk, S., & Lenz, W. (2010). Infection, media, and capitalism: From early modern plagues to postmodern zombies. *Journal for Early Modern Cultural Studies*, *10*(2), 126–147.

Brian Campbell. (October 19, 2021). "A Call for Papers Template for You to Use". Retrieved November 29, 2021, from Ex Ordo website.

Brookfield, S. D. (2011). Addressing feedback from reviewers and editors. In T. S. Rocco & T. Hatcher (Eds.), *The Handbook of Scholarly Writing and Publishing* (pp. 251–261). San Francisco: Jossey-Bass.

Chen, S. (2007). Extracurricular reading habits of college students in Taiwan. *Journal of Adolescent & Adult Literacy*, *50*(8), 642–653.

DeLoach, S. B., Perry-Sizemore, E., & Borg, M. O. (2012). Creating quality undergraduate research programs in economics: How, when, where (and why). *The American Economist*, *57*(1), 96–110.

Depling. (n.d.). "Depling 2021: 6th International Conference on Dependency Linguistics". Retrieved November 29, 2021, from WikiCFP website.

Dix, A. (2008). Theoretical analysis and theory creation. In P. Cairns & A. Cox (Eds.), *Research Methods for Human-computer Interaction* (pp.175–195). Cambridge: Cambridge University Press.

Dromi, S. M., & Illouz, E. (2010). Recovering morality: Pragmatic sociology and literary studies. *New Literary History*, *41*(2), 351–369.

Editage Insights. (n.d.). "A template for responding to peer reviewer comments". Retrieved August 7, 2021, from Editage Insights website.

Editage Insights. (October 14, 2014). "Tracking your manuscript status in journal submission systems". Retrieved August 13, 2021, from Editage Insights website.

Educationconf. (n.d.). "Conference Call for Papers". Retrieved August 21, 2021, from EDUCATIONCONF website.

Efron, S. E., & Ravid, R. (2018). Writing the literature review: A practical guide. New York: Guilford Press.

Englander, K. (2013). *Writing and Publishing Science Research Papers in English: A Global Perspective*. New York: Springer.

F1000Research. (n.d.). "Peer review examples". Retrieved August 7, 2021, from F1000Research website.

Fatiloro, O. F., Adesola, O. A., & Adewumi, O. M. (2017). A survey on the reading habits among colleges of education students in the information age. *Journal of Education and Practice*, *8*(8), 106–110.

Fine Arts Conference. (n.d.). "The 8th International Conference on Arts and Humanities 2021". Retrieved August 22, 2021, from Fine Arts Conference website.

Henan University. (October 10, 2016). "Call for Papers". Retrieved September 21, 2021, from Henan University School of Economics website.

Jasso, G. (1988). Principles of theoretical analysis. *Sociological Theory*, *6*(1), 1–20.

Joët, G., Usher, E. L., & Bressoux, P. (2011). Sources of self-efficacy: An investigation of elementary school students in France. *Journal of Educational Psychology*, *103*(3), 649.

Jong, N. H. (2018). Fluency in second language testing: Insights from different disciplines. *Language Assessment Quarterly, 15*(3), 237–254.

Karadeniz, A., & Remzi, C. (2015). Research on book reading habits and media literacy of students at the faculty of education. *Social and Behavioral Sciences, 174*(1), 4058–4067.

References

Kates, A. W., Wu, H., & Coryn, C. L. (2018). The effects of mobile phone use on academic performance: A meta-analysis. *Computers & Education, 127*, 107–112.

Kato, M., & Akinobu, N. (2021). The impact of subject-specific competencies and reading habits on the income of Japanese business and economics graduates. *International Journal of Educational Development, 81*(1),102346.

Kim, S. (March 12, 2018). "12 Tips for Building a Conference Agenda". Retrieved August 22, 2021, from Bizzabo website.

Lyubomirsky, S., King, L., & Diener, E. (2005). The benefits of frequent positive affect: Does happiness lead to success? *Psychological Bulletin, 131*(6), 803–855.

McArthur, J. (2021). The inclusive university: A critical theory perspective using a recognition-based approach. *Social Inclusion, 9*(3), 6–15.

Merkel, W. (2021). Collage of confusion: An analysis of one university's multiple plagiarism policies. *System, 96*, 102399.

Nahata, M. C., & Sorkin, E. M. (2019). Responding to manuscript reviewer and editor comments. *Annals of Pharmacotherapy, 53*(9), 959–961.

Neuman, N. (2019). On the engagement with social theory in food studies: Cultural symbols and social practices. *Food, Culture & Society, 22*(1), 78–94.

Paltridge, B., & Starfield, S. (2007). *Thesis and Dissertation Writing in a Second Language.* London: Routledge.

Perucca, G. (2019). Residents' satisfaction with cultural city life: Evidence from EU cities. *Applied Research in Quality of Life, 14*(2), 461–478.

Proofed. (May 22, 2020). "5 Tips on How to Write a Call for Papers". Retrieved September 21, 2021, from Proofed website.

Rocco, T. S. (2011). Reasons to write, writing opportunities, and other considerations. In T. S. Rocco & T. Hatcher (Eds.), *The Handbook of Scholarly Writing and Publishing* (pp.3–12). San Francisco: Jossey-Bass.

Scholastica. (February 13, 2020). "7 e-mail templates for common peer review correspondences". Retrieved August 7, 2021, from Scholastica website.

Taylor & Francis Online. (n.d.). "News, Offers and Calls for Papers". Retrieved August

15, 2021, from Taylor & Francis Online Website.

Template. (n.d.). "What Should Be in the Conference Program?". Retrieved August 22, 2021, from Template website.

Thompson, P., & Kamler, B. (2013). *Writing for Peer Reviewed Journals*. New York: Routledge.

University of Adelaide. (2014). "Introductions and conclusions". Retrieved August 7, 2021, from University of Adelaide website.

Wang, G. T., & Park, K. (2016). *Student Research and Report Writing: From Topic Selection to the Complete Paper*. Oxford: Wiley-Blackwell.

Wang, P., Chiu, D. K. W., Ho, K. K. W., & Lo, P. (2016). Why read it on your mobile device? Change in reading habit of electronic magazines for university students. *The Journal of Academic Librarianship*, *42*(6), 664–669.

Wang, Y., & Li, W. (2021). Cognitive restructuring in the multilingual mind: Language-specific effects on processing efficiency of caused motion events in Cantonese-English-Japanese speakers. *Bilingualism: Language and Cognition*, *11*(4), 1–16.

Wei, L. (2018). Translanguaging as a practical theory of language. *Applied Linguistics*, *39*(1), 9–30.

Wright, R. (2019). Lexical bundles in stand-alone literature reviews: Sections, frequencies, and functions. *English for Specific Purposes*, *54*, 1–14.

Zhang, L., & Tsung, L. (2021). Learning Chinese as a second language in China: Positive emotions and enjoyment. *System*, *96*, 102410.

Zhou, S., & Rose, H. (2021). Self-regulated listening of students at transition from high school to an English medium instruction (EMI) transnational university in China. *System, 103*, 102644.